John Arthur Phillips

Thompson's turkey and other Christmas tales and poems

John Arthur Phillips

Thompson's turkey and other Christmas tales and poems

ISBN/EAN: 9783741193668

Manufactured in Europe, USA, Canada, Australia, Japa

Cover: Foto ©Andreas Hilbeck / pixelio.de

Manufactured and distributed by brebook publishing software (www.brebook.com)

John Arthur Phillips

Thompson's turkey and other Christmas tales and poems

THOMPSON'S TURKEY,

AND OTHER

Christmas Tales, Poems, &c.,

BY

J. A. PHILLIPS.

Author of "From Bad to Worse," "Hard to Beat," &c.

Montreal:
OHN LOVELL, 23 AND 25 ST. NICHOLAS STREET.
1873.

Entered according to Act of Parliament of Canada, in the year one thousand eight hundred and seventy-three, by JOHN A. PHILLIPS, in the office of the Minister of Agriculture and Sta'istics at Ottawa.

To My Noble Self,

AS BEING THE MOST CONSTANT AND DEVOTED ADMIRER
I EVER HAD,

THIS BOOK IS,

BY SPECIAL PERMISSION,

Respectfully Dedicated:

IN GRATEFUL ACKNOWLEDGMENT OF MANY KINDNESSES
RECEIVED DURING

A LONG ACQUAINTANCESHIP,

AND IN THE EARNEST HOPE OF FUTURE FAVORS.

J. A. PHILLIPS.

PREFACE.

It is the customary thing to apologise for writing a book. I don't want to apologise. If I have written anything needing apology I am unconscious of it; when I am it will be time enough to apologise. What I want to say is, that I have not aimed very high in this volume, and I hope I have not struck very low; I have simply tried to write a few amusing tales suitable for the Christmas fireside, containing nothing offensive and some things which might be conducive to good morals; if I have succeeded in that I am content; and I only hope that everyone who reads what I have written will be content also. And that is just why I have written this preface. I would like to know whether my readers are pleased or not; and, therefore, I am going to take a liberty. I ask everyone who reads this book to send me his or her candid opinion of it to my Post Office address, Box 704½, Montreal.

It will not give much trouble, and it will not cost much—only one cent by post card—and it will afford me great gratification to get criticisms from the people who read the book. If I have pleased them I should like to know it; and if I have made a fool of myself I should like to be made acquainted with the fact, so as to save me from further folly.

JNO. A. PHILLIPS.

Montreal, 1st December, 1873.

CONTENTS.

PREFACE	5
THOMPSON'S TURKEY	9
THE CHRISTMAS ANTHEM	43
THE POLICEMAN'S CHRISTMAS	63
OUT OF THE GUTTER	105
JONES, THE LAWYER	131
OUT OF THE SNOW	191
CHRISTMAS IN THE FLIES	211
POETRY:—	
A CHRISTMAS PRAYER	239
DREAMLAND	240
THE OLD FOLK'S CHRISTMAS	241
MUSIC	244
GHOSTS ON THE WINDOW PANE	246
THE CHILD'S GRAVE	247
GOD IN NATURE	249
THE DYING CHILD	251
THE FACTORY GIRL	253
PLEASANT REVERIES	255

THOMPSON'S TURKEY.

CHAPTER I.

HOW THOMPSON GOT THE TURKEY

It wasn't Thompson's fault.

I take this the earliest possible opportunity, to give it as my free, candid and disinterested opinion that it wasn't Thompson's fault. I am quite well aware of the fact that there were people before the time who said it was Thompson's fault; I am quite well aware of the fact that there were people at the time who said it was Thompson's fault; I am quite well aware of the fact that there were people after the time who said it was Thompson's fault; I am quite well aware of the fact that there are people who even to the present day maintain that it was Thompson's fault; but I never did believe it was Thompson's fault, and I never will.

The fact is Thompson couldn't help it.

I know very well there were people at the time who said that Thompson could have helped it; I know very well that there were people after the time who said

Thompson could have helped it; I know very well
there are people now who still assert that Thompson
could have helped it; but I never did believe Thompson could help it, and I never will.

And, after all, what was it that people said was
Thompson's fault; and what was it that people said
Thompson could have helped doing?

Why, getting married; that was all!

I never could see, and I never will see that it was
Thompson's fault to get married; other people do it,
why shouldn't Thompson? I never could see, and I
never will see that Thompson could have helped it;
other people can't help it, and why should Thompson?

And then everybody wanted to marry Winnie
Dumsie, why shouldn't Thompson? But, Winnie—her
name was Winnetta, but we always called her Winnie
for short—didn't want to marry everybody; she didn't
even want to marry me, although I was ready and
willing to marry her several times over if necessary;
she didn't want to marry old Flailflax, the wealthy
linen draper, although he did own a big house on
the mountain side, and was reported to have so much
money in the bank, that an extra vault had had to be
built on purpose to hold it all; she didn't want to marry
young Grunter, the pork packer, although he was
always as sleek and smooth as if just freshly rubbed
with some of his own grease, and his father was said
to have left him enough money to pack every pig in
Canada, himself included; she didn't want to marry

the Rev. Mr. Maypole, the new curate of St. Fashionable's, although he was so upright, and dressed so nicely, and read prayers " beautifully"—so the other girls said—and gave the old women snuff to brace up their nerves—the girls all said that was "so charitable"—and did a thousand and one things which always made unmarried curates so agreeable to the female portion of the congregation of St. Fashionable's ; the fact is Winnie wanted to marry Thompson, and she did it.

Young ladies sometimes will do such things, whether their parents like it or not; and, therefore, as Winnie had made up her mind to marry Thompson, she did marry him, and I say it wasn't Thompson's fault, and he couldn't help it.

There were other reasons why Thompson couldn't help it. Winnie Dumsie was one of the sweetest, most lovable little bits of femininity that ever set a poor male mortal crazy ; she was so rosy, so joyous, so artless, so natural, so piquant, so winning that nobody could help loving her ; I couldn't, how could Thompson?

Then she and Thompson had grown up together from childhood ; even when she was a little thing in short frocks and frills round her pantalets nobody could help stealing apples, and cakes, and sweetmeats, and other things for her, and tearing their clothes climbing for flowers to please her, and fighting each other on her account, and wanting to kiss her and being too bashful to do it; I couldn't, and how could Thompson?

She always looked to me like a lump of sugar, and I was not at all astonished when Thompson put her in his cup of life to sweeten it for all time; I wasn't astonished, but everybody else was.

You see this was the way of it. Winnie was rich; old Dumsie, her father, was a large dealer in small-wares, pins and needles and such things, and a good deal of money had stuck to old Dumsie's fingers by the aid of pins and needles and such things. He was a proud man, was old Dumsie; very fond of his only child, and very fond of talking of his " connections in the old country"—Rumor said he had been a pot-boy in Dublin in his youthful days, but Rumor might have lied as she very often does; and everybody knows that every Irishman, out of Ireland, is either an Irish king, or the descendant of one. It has often struck me that kings in Ireland must have been very plentiful at some time, and that they must have been amongst the earliest immigrants, which would, of course, account for so many of their descendants being found on this side of the Atlantic; be that as it may, Dumsie was the lineal descendant of an Irish king, so he said, and had a right to be proud, which he was, whether he had the right or not.

Being proud, Dumsie, of course, would not hear of Thompson for a son-in-law, for Thompson was poor; in fact, Thompson was only a clerk in old Dumsie's

fore, and although Dumsie and Thompson's father had
been great friends, and Dumsie himself had been very
kind to Thompson since his father's death, still he
could not have dreamed of giving Winnie to him.

Nor was poverty his only objection to Thompson;
no, that might have been overcome; but it was Thompson's name, that could not be overcome.

You see old Dumsie had studied genealogies and
derivations very deeply—that was how he found out
that he was the descendant of an Irish king—and he
informed Thompson that his name was very plebeian:
in fact, old Dumsie went so far as to say that there
was no such thing as a Thompson with a p. He
argued, and with considerable show of correctness,
that the name, as a surname, was derived from the
Christian name Thomas, and had been originally
written Thomas' son, and applied to a younger member of the family as indicating that he was a son of
the original Thomas; that on the general adoption of
surnames the apostrophe and one s were dropped,
and the name written Thomason, which in due course
of time had become changed to Thomson, or Tomson; but Thompson—with a p—he looked on as a
base impostor of a name, and triumphantly asked
'how did the p get in?'

Of course, Thompson did not like to hear his name
abused, and retaliated on Dumsie by telling him that
his, Dumsie's, name was originally Drumstick, and
that the r, t and k had got knocked out of the name

at various stages of its transmission from the Irish
king to the present owner; but that only made
Dumsie mad, and when Thompson told him that he
loved Winnie, and asked his consent to their union
when he was able to support her—for he was a proud
fellow, was Thompson, and didn't want to marry
Winnie for her money, but because he loved her—
old Dumsie poured out all the vials of his wrath, and
vowed that if she married Thompson he would cut
her off with a farthing, so that the p in her name
should not even stand for a penny.

That was a terrible time for Thompson; of course
he lost his place in old Dumsie's store; and, of
course, old Dumsie forbid his seeing or speaking to
Winnie again; and, of course, Winnie and Thompson
used to meet each other on the sly and vow eternal
constancy and all that sort of thing; and, of course,
they used to write to each other every day, and I used
to deliver the notes without old Dumsie suspecting
me—for he rather liked me and thought I was going
to marry Winnie, but Winnie didn't love me and
did love Thompson, and although I liked Thompson
very well, I didn't care to marry a girl who loved him
and didn't love me.

Thompson soon got another place, but it was not
as good as the one he had lost, and the chances of
matrimony seemed further off than ever; but things
are often nearest to us when they seem furthest off.
It was summer when old Dumsie discharged Thomp

son, and the lovers agreed to wait five years for each other; but, somehow as the cold weather came on, and it was not so pleasant waiting in Viger Garden, or Victoria Square to meet each other, both parties suddenly changed their minds, and one morning early in December Thompson entered my office in a very excited manner and asked me to come and see him married.

Thompson and I were always very friendly, although we did love the same girl; it wasn't his fault if Winnie cared for him and not for me, so I couldn't blame Thompson, could I? So I went to see them married, and gave away the bride, I did and I kissed her next after Thompson, I did; and it made me feel as if a frozen poker had been run down my back when I thought it was the last time I would ever kiss her. But I didn't let them see that I felt it, and offered to take Winnie's note to her father asking for forgiveness and deliver it in person.

It was as great a refresher to me as a shower bath to see old Dumsie get mad when I told him what had happened; he turned so red in the face I thought he would go off in a fit of apoplexy, and I half wished he would, for I knew he had made a will leaving Winnie his heiress, and if he died right off he would not have time to alter it; but he didn't know enough to die decently, he must live to make himself disagreeable, and so, after a while he recovered himself, and the first thing he said was:

"Phillips, you're a fool."

I told him that possibly he might be correct, but I did not think it polite to state it quite so plainly. He did not mind that at all, but repeated the obnoxious expression prefacing the word fool with a very objectionable adjective which made me so angry that for a moment a desperate desire to seize him by the throat, choke him to death, and say he died of apoplexy on hearing the news, came over me; but I thought of the marks I should leave on the neck, of the coroner's jury, of a trial for murder, of a rope and other unpleasant things, and stifling my indignation contented myself with saying "you're another."

But if I stifled my wrath old Dumsie didn't stifle his; he raved terribly, and used shocking bad language for so old a man; he swore he would never forgive Winnie, that he would drive Thompson to despair, and so many more dreadful things, that I was forced to leave him, and the old fool made a new will that same day and took himself off on an express train that night no one knew whither.

Poor Thompson had a hard time of it at first; his salary was small, and Winnie had been accustomed to so many luxuries that it seemed a shame to deprive her of. But they both put their shoulders bravely to the wheel, and it was astonishing how well they got on. Winnie would not hear of boarding, and determined to keep house herself. They got the upper part of a house in a cheap and quiet by-street and it was surprising how nicely and cosily they fitted it up, considering their limited means. Thompson always used to say that he could never have done it but for the timely aid of a kind friend; but Thompson, although a good fellow, is rather foolish on some subjects, and sometimes talks about things that he ought not to speak of to everybody.

How happy they were; how much they loved each other, and how they cheered and helped each other nobody knows better than I; and nobody felt it more than I did the first evening I spent with them and sat by the fire crying, half with pleasure, half with pain, like the great fool that I am, and swearing all the time that it was a splinter from the crackling wood which had flown into my eye and made it water. Very happy and very contented they were, and very hard Thompson worked to sustain his humble home.

He wasn't a fool, wasn't Thompson; far from it, he was a clever sort of chap, and could do lots of things besides wait behind a counter and sell ribbons and things to young ladies. He was a well educated fellow, was Thompson, and could write poetry so nicely that the girls were always wanting him to write in their Albums; and so, when old Dumsie discharged him, Thompson thought he would turn his talents to account and he sent some of his writings to the American papers, for the Canadian papers were willing enough to publish, but very unwilling to pay, and as Thompson was writing for bread and butter he could not afford that kind of business.

Very nice stories did Thompson write, and his *nom de plume* of "Phontoms"—anagram of Thompson, for he would stick to his name—soon got to be well known and liked. But at first he got very little pay for his productions, and what he did get, added to his salary, was scarce enough to keep Winnie and himself, even with the exercise of great economy.

It was about three weeks before Christmas that they were married and commenced housekeeping, and Winnie had set her heart on giving a "party" at Christmas and asking some of her old friends to come and witness her triumphs of housekeeping; but it was a great undertaking, and had to be calmly considered and gone about in a serious manner.

Dinners are expensive things, and economical as she tried to be, Winnie found that the plainest fare she could afford to set before the half dozen friends she had invited would make a deep hole in her scanty purse; and very little would be left to provide refreshments for those who had been asked to come after dinner and spend the evening.

"I don't see how I can manage it," said Winnie, pushing back her hair and looking up from a little red book, in which she had been making some entries, at her husband who was busy writing at the centre table; " Do you think we could do without any dessert, Charlie, dear!" I forgot to mention before that Thompson's other name was Charles, but I suppose it don't make much difference.

"Do without dessert, darling? well, it wouldn't look very well for Christmas; but you know best, if we can't afford it, don't do it. I have given you all the money I have, and I wont run in debt; a man in debt never belongs to himself, and I mean to belong to myself if nothing else does."

"Nothing else?" inquired an arch voice, as a pair of loving arms were wound round his neck and a dainty little form threw itself into his lap with an impetuous rush which sent all the papers flying.

"Well nothing worth speaking about; of course, you don't count now, you are part of me, and the law does not recognize you as a good and chattel."

"But do you recognize me as a good? I don't like to be called a chattel."

"The best good in the world to me;" and then there was a little joyous squeeze, and a great deal of nonsense was said, and the ink bottle escaped being overturned on the new table cover by a miracle before common-sense conversation was resumed. They were very nonsensical people, were Thompson and his young wife, and they were not yet through their honeymoon you must remember.

"But about the dinner, Charlie," resumed Winnie presently. "I've stretched the money as far as it will go and if I have dessert there wont be enough for the turkey; we ought to have a turkey, oughtn't we?"

"I suppose so; people do generally have a turkey for Christmas dinner; but if we can't afford it we must do without it. I wish we had the one I have described in that Christmas story I sent to Harpers."

"We can't eat a turkey out of a Christmas story," said Winnie, sententiously. "We might as well try an entire banquet out of 'The Arabian Nights' at once."

"Then Phil"—Winnie always would abbreviate my name somehow—"and the others must be content with roast beef and plum pudding; I'm going to make a plum pudding, Charlie, for it wouldn't be Christmas without it."

"Say you are going to try to make one, puss, but don't expect me to eat any of it; I have too much respect for my digestive organs."

"Then you shan't have a bit of it, sir, for your impudence, and Phil shall have the whole of it."

"Poor Phil, I pity him," sighed Thompson with mock concern for which he got the tiniest possible slap on the ear and the sweetest possible kiss on the lips.

"Now then, puss, jump down and let me go on with my writing," and so the turkey was dropped for the time being.

But Thompson did not forget it; he thought of it several times the next day, and determined to stretch a point, if possible, and get a turkey if only to surprise and please Winnie.

Luck favored Thompson, and two days before Christmas he received a polite note from Harpers enclosing a cheque for twenty-five dollars for the accepted

Christmas story, and offering to purchase more of his productions.

This was the largest sum he had ever received for an article, and a proud man was Thompson as he walked into a neighboring broker's office and got his cheque cashed. "One ten and the rest in ones, if you please," said Thompson, thinking how he would surprise Winnie by presenting her with the turkey, and then raining one dollar bills on her afterwards The broker gave him the money, and smiled quite pleasantly as he said,

"Making your fortune fast now, eh, Thompson, my boy? That's right. A merry Christmas to you," and Thompson felt himself grow half an inch taller as he walked out.

It was a busy day at the store that day, and it was quite late when Thompson took down his overcoat to start for home where he knew tea was ready and Winnie anxiously expecting him; he was a little late already, and, besides, he had the turkey to buy.

"Wait a minute, Thompson," called out the junior partner as Thompson passed the office, "I have something to say to you before you go."

And so he had to wait another five minutes; but the "something" proved very pleasant to hear, for the junior partner told him that the head of the firm —who was the junior partner's father—was very much pleased with the way he had conducted himself since he had been in the employ of the firm, and presented him with a cheque for fifty dollars, and promised him an increase of one hundred dollars salary next year.

Happy Thompson! He almost kissed the junior partner on the spot, and with difficulty restrained himself from executing a little impromptu dance of joy; but he managed to stammer out a few words of thanks and reserved his terpsichorean performance until he should have reached home.

"That's right," said the junior partner approvingly to what Thompson had said, "you always take an interest in your employers' business, and be sure they will take an interest in you. Here," he continued to a cash-boy who was passing, "take that to the cashier and ask him to give me small bills, ones or twos, for it. I am going off to Toronto to-night, Thompson," he went on as the boy departed on his errand. "I shall eat my Christmas dinner there, and be away three or four days; look after the store for me a bit while I am gone."

"The cashier says he aint got no small bills, sir," said the cash-boy returning and holding out a ten dollar bill to the junior partner.

"That's very provoking," said that gentleman, "I have nothing but tens and twenties and I want to buy some car tickets. Do you happen to have any small bills, Thompson?"

Of course Thompson had, and he handed ten of them to the junior partner, buttoned up the ten dollar bill with the cheque and his other money, and went on his way rejoicing to buy the turkey.

CHAPTER II.

HOW THE TURKEY GOT THOMPSON.

It was a hard turkey to buy, and took some time to select. Thompson had never done any marketing before, and had an idea that it was a very easy matter to walk into the market, select a turkey, pay for it and carry it off with him; but when he got there he saw so many turkeys it was quite distracting to make a selection, and the clatter of the poultry vendors so confused him that he had nearly invested in a scraggy looking goose when he was touched on the shoulder and a laughing voice said at his elbow,

"Ha, ha, Mr. Married Man, doing your own marketing already; where is the gude wife?"

"Oh, Mrs. Westerville, I am so glad to see you. I was just—that is I want to—well I was trying to buy a turkey."

"And very nearly purchased a goose. O you men are not fit to be trusted marketing by yourselves; why didn't Winnie come with you?"

"You see I intend this for a surprise."

"And you would have surprised her I have no doubt, if you had taken her home a goose and called it a turkey. Let me make your purchases for you."

"Oh, thank you. I am afraid I shall make a mess of it if I try it alone."

"Of course you will; men always do. And how is Winnie? I havn't seen her since your marriage. Oh what naughty people you were to get married on the sly, and not even send me a piece of wedding cake."

"Winnie is quite well, thanks, and will be glad to see you if you don't mind calling in rather queer quarters. We are not very rich, you know, and poor people can't be very particular where they live."

"Never mind your 'queer quarters,' Mr. Poor Man, I'll come and see you if you will give me your address. There, will that turkey do?" holding out a large plump bird which she had poked in the breast, and pinched in the back, and pulled by the legs, and squeezed by the bill, and satisfied herself was young and tender.

"That will do very nicely indeed, thank you. What is the price?" to the stall keeper.

"Seven and sixpence."

"A dollar and a half!" cried Mrs. Westerville in pretended astonishment. "It's downright robbery. I paid a dollar for one only yesterday; these market people always take advantage of you men, they see you know nothing about it, and cheat you in the most barefaced manner."

After a little haggling the turkey was purchased for a dollar and a quarter, and Thompson having bought some vegetables which he thought Winnie

might want for the dinner, and some grapes which
he intended for her own special eating, changed one
of his ten dollar bills so as to get plenty of small
change again, and having loaded himself up like a
pack horse trotted homeward happy.

Very much delighted was Winnie, and very scepti-
cal about the quality of the turkey until told that
Mrs. Westerville had bought it, and then she suddenly
subsided before the superior wisdom of that matron
of nearly a year's standing. Very much delighted
was Winnie, and a very pleasant, happy evening they
passed, she sitting on his lap eating grapes and occasionally holding one between her rosy lips and making
him take it from them with his—I told you they were
a very silly couple; and very animated was Winnie
with her details of the grand preparations—in a small
way—which she had made for the eventful Christmas;
very merry and joyous she was, and a little inquisitive
too, for she asked Thompson more than once where
he had got all the money from to buy "turkeys"—
she said turkeys, although there was but one—"and
grapes, and vegetables and all manner of things."

But he was a dark and mysterious Thompson that
night, and for the first time in his life deceived his
darling a little; for he was a plotting and a scheming
Thompson also, and was laying a deep plan for surprising his little wife the next night; and so he
answered evasively that he had "found that he had
more money than he expected, and could afford a little

extra expenses," and so put her off with a kiss. Very happy and very merry were they, and many a little joke was cracked about the turkey.

Next morning Thompson was up bright and early and off to business with a light heart; and several times during the day he caught himself whistling snatches of gay little songs as he attended on the customers who thronged the store. A little before dinner time he got his cheque changed by the cashier, receiving as many small bills as that gentleman could spare—it was wonderful how much Thompson seemed to want small bills—and four tens.

As soon as the clock struck twelve he ran out ostensibly to dinner, but that was surely only an excuse, for he had told Winnie he would be too busy to come home and that he would get something to eat down town. Nowhere near home, nor any restaurant did Thompson go, but right to old Dumsie's store in Notre Dame street, and entered it as large as life just as if he was going to buy the whole store and pay for it on the spot.

But he didn't want the whole store, he only wanted a very small portion of some of the goods in the store; for be it known that amongst the "small wares" in which old Dumsie dealt were sundry articles of jewellery, and one of these articles, a dead gold brooch with a small amethyst in it, Thompson had set his heart on possessing and presenting to Winnie as a Christmas present. Very glad were his old fellow

clerks to see him, and many a merry little joke was
passed about his "changed appearance since he became a double man," and other kindred pleasantries ;
and when he pulled out two ten dollar bills to pay for
the brooch—the price was twelve dollars and a half
—one of the clerks began to chaff him and asked if
he had "struck a mine," or "robbed a bank," or
"made them himself," and such like playful questions
And when he went to the cashier's desk to get his
change there sat old Dumsie himself, who had
returned suddenly that morning from nobody knew
where, looking as cross as he could, and he never said
a word to Thompson, or as much as look at him ; but
he put on his spectacles and peered very suspiciously
at the bills as if he thought they were bad, and he
grunted in a disappointed sort of way as he threw
them into the drawer and counted out the change.
Very cross and savage indeed did old Dumsie look,
but Thompson never heeded him, his heart was too
full of joy for him to mind how old Dumsie looked ;
and he went whistling gaily out of the shop and
turned into a tobacconist's, where he was known, and
enquired the price of a handsome little meerschaum
cigar holder which he wished to present to a stupid,
blundering, foolish sort of a friend of his whom he
was pleased to think himself under some sort of
obligation to.

He changed another ten-dollar bill at the tobacconist's, and after he had received the change counted

out twenty-five dollars in one-dollar bills and put that
away carefully in one pocket, and laughed slily as he
did so, did that artful Thompson, and put the remaining twenty-two dollars—two tens, and a two
into another pocket ; then he went back to business,
and every now and then during the afternoon he
chuckled to himself in a satisfied sort of way.

As Thompson had not gone home to dinner he was
allowed an hour and a half for supper, and he went off
sharp at six whistling all the way and in the best
possible humor with himself. But all the good spirits
in which he had been all day were as nothing to his
uproarious hilarity when he heard Winnie's little
shriek of delight at the production of the brooch, and
saw her look of wonder when he pelted the one
dollar bills at her, one at a time to make them last
longer ; and then she climbed on his lap and made
him tell her all about it ; and beautiful castles in the
air they built of the great things which they were to
do when Thompson had become a world renowned
author and made an immense fortune—authors
always do make immense fortunes, in books you
know, although they very seldom do in real life.

Very merrily and gaily they chatted away without
thinking of supper, and Thompson's hour and a half
was almost all gone when he suddenly remembered
that he was very hungry and fell to with a good
appetite.

But Thompson was not destined to enjoy his supper

that night, for he had scarcely taken two bites out of the round of toast when there was a great knocking at the door, and on Winnie's opening it three men pushed past her and entered the room.

Thompson knew them in a moment, and rose in astonishment; they were old Dumsie, a detective— whom Thompson knew by sight—and a policeman in uniform.

"What does this intrusion mean?" asked Thompson looking with surprise at the intruders, while Winnie, with that instinctive feeling which women have that one they love is in danger, came to his side and put her arm around him as if to shield him.

"There he is," said old Dumsie savagely, "catch him before he runs away."

"I'm very sorry, Mr. Thompson," said the detective, who was a mild eyed, gentlemanly looking man, "will you step outside for a minute?" and he glanced at Winnie.

"No, he won't," she interrupted, before Thompson could speak: "Whatever you have to say you can say before me. What is it?"

"There is a little trouble about some one passing counterfeit bills," said the detective, "and he's wanted down at the Station;" somehow he didn't like to tell that brave looking little woman that a charge of passing counterfeit bills had been made against her husband.

"Tell the truth," said old Dumsie sharply, "he's

arrested for passing counterfeit notes ; the woman he bought a turkey from last night has made a charge against him, and he passed two on me to day. I'll make an affidavit to-morrow. The rascal to steal my daughter and then try to rob me ; he ought to be hung."

"It's all a confounded lie," shouted Thompson taking a step towards old Dumsie in so fierce a manner as to make that gentleman skip nimbly behind the policeman. "I know nothing about any counterfeit bills; all the money I have had for the last two days I got from Mr. Stamps, the broker, and from the cashier of our store."

"Well, perhaps you'll be able to make it all right, sir," said the detective kindly ; " but if you'd take my advice you wouldn't say much now. I may have to use it as evidence against you."

"Use whatever you please," said Thompson savagely. "I've got nothing to conceal in the matter: Take me anywhere you please at once and let me explain this matter."

"Oh, yes," said old Dumsie peeping cautiously from behind the policeman, "he can explain, of course! He can explain where he got the money to ⟨bu⟩y turkeys"—*he* said turkeys too, although there ⟨was⟩ but one—" and give dinner parties, and buy brooches, and throw bank notes about like this," and he pointed to the heap of dollar bills which Winnie had left on the table.

"I will explain nothing, except before the proper authorities," said Thompson calmly: "I am ready to go at once. I scarcely thought, Mr. Dumsic," he continued, turning to that gentleman, "that your spite against me would have carried you as far as this. May God forgive you the injustice you do me, and the pain you cause your own flesh and blood."

"It isn't him," said the detective, "it's the poultry dealer who made the complaint; she found out this morning that the bill was bad, and I went to the store to find you. The cashier told me you were here, and as I was coming along I met Mr. Dumsic who told me you had passed two counterfeits on him; he hasn't made any charge yet."

"Yes, I have," cried old Dumsic, "I make it now, and I will swear to it to-morrow morning."

"Let us go," said Thompson reaching for his hat "I want to get this thing settled at once. Cheer up darling," he continued to Winnie, "it is nothing serious, I will be back soon."

"Do you think I am going to let you go alone? No, Charlie; I'm your wife, and wherever you go I go with you. I know this is a base, wicked calumny, a plot to separate us, but it shan't; no matter where they take you, they must take me too."

Her face was very pale, but her lip never trembled, and her eyes shone bright and trusting up to Thompson's.

"Stay where you are," said old Dumsic speaking

to Winnie, and looking at her for the first time. "I am your father, I will take care of you, you shan't go to prison with this fellow."

"Father, I always tried to be a good dutiful daughter to you; I loved you dearly until you endeavored to make my life miserable and forced me to an act of disobedience; I am happy now in the love of the man who loves me, and I cannot and will not leave him."

She disengaged herself from Thompson's arms and quickly put on her bonnet and cloak.

"Come, we are ready now. Can you go round by St. Urbain street?" she asked the detective. "I have a friend there I should like to consult."

"All right, ma'am," replied the detective, "we can make it in the way."

"You'll go quietly, sir?" he inquired of Thompson.

"Certainly."

"Come along then," he said, and walked out of the room followed by Thompson and Winnie, which conduct so astonished the policeman who was a Frenchman, and had understood nothing of what had passed and who had come to assist at arresting somebody, that he seized old Dumsic by the collar and led him off in triumph.

CHAPTER III.

HOW THE TURKEY GOT EATEN.

I do like to enjoy a good smoke. I don't know anything more calculated to make a man feel at peace with his washerwoman and the rest of mankind than to lie in an easy chair, with one's slippered feet duly elevated, and slowly and luxuriously inhale peace, comfort and bliss through the medium of a well seasoned pipe, after having partaken of a good hearty supper. I always did take especial pleasure in my after-supper smoke, and on this particular Christmas Eve of which I have been writing, I derived more than my usual comfort from my favorite clay; for it was charged with primest of Latakia, and I had my most particular friend and boon companion, Jack Rainforth, sitting opposite me pulling away industriously at an ancient briar, and varying his occupation occasionally by mixing a little warm brandy and water and telling funny stories.

He was a wonderful fellow, was Jack, and knew a little of everything; he was a bit of a lawyer, and a bit of a doctor, and something of an author, and had been a strolling player, and could tell lots of funny stories about "the profession" as he called it, and was always full of good humor, so that it was quite a treat to have him for a companion. I always considered it a treat to have Jack with me, and thought myself particularly lucky this evening to have him all to myself so that I could enjoy him alone and not have to share him with others. Jack was just telling me a capital story about a dog which belonged to a friend of his when there was a sudden knock at the door, and before I had time to call out " come in," it opened and Thompson, and Winnie, and the detective entered.

I never was more astonished in my life, and sat stupidly staring at them with my feet still on the table, quite forgetting that I had dropped one of my slippers and that there was a great hole in the toe of my sock, until Thompson's voice roused me.

" Phil, old fellow," he said, " I have been arrested for passing counterfeit money, and am on my way to the police station, will you come with me; perhaps I shall want a friend to help me out of the scrape."

" Go with you, old boy, why of course I will," I cried, trying in my excitement to pull on my pipe under the delusion that it was a boot and burning my toe so that it made me jump. " But what do you mean? tell me all about it."

Then Thompson told us what has been related in the last chapter, and we all stood silent for a moment when he had finished, looking at each other; it was Jack who spoke first, and his words made us all start.

" Where is the cashier?" asked Jack fixing his eye on the detective.

"He was at the store half an hour ago," answered the detective looking as blank as a blank cartridge after it has been exploded.

But it wouldn't do, Jack kept his eye on him and saw that he saw that Jack saw that he saw what Jack meant.

"You won't find him there now," said Jack. "You gave him warning by calling at the store, and by this time he is on his way to Rouse's Point. You all go down to the Station and wait for me, I will just go round by the store and then join you. Come with me, Phil."

Jack and I went to the store where Thompson was employed, and found one of the other clerks at the cashier's desk.

"Where is Mr. Moyson," that was the cashier's name, I asked.

"He's been gone about half an hour, sir; he said he didn't feel well, and left me in his place for the rest of the evening."

"Did he lock the safe?" asked Jack.

"No," said the clerk, rather surprised at the question, "he counted what money he had taken and put it away, leaving me to lock up when I got through."

"Just look in the safe and see if the money is there," said Jack.

The clerk looked very much astonished, but turned to the safe, and in a minute he came back with a blanched face, and said,

" I think Mr. Moyson has taken it home with him;
it isn't there."

"I think he has," replied Jack dryly. " Do you
know where he lives?"

" No. —, McGill College Avenue."

" Thank you," and Jack hurried out of the store.
" It's just as plain as it can be," he continued, when
we were on the street, " this fellow has been plant-
ing a lot of bad bills by the aid of his position, and he
gave those tons to Thompson ; and now, seeing that
his game is up he has collared all the cash he can lay
his hands on and bolted." Jack used a great deal of
slang sometimes, especially when he was excited.

" Perhaps he hasn't gone yet, he might be at his
boarding house packing up," said I.

" I intend going there at once," replied Jack hailing
a sleigh.

We reached McGill College Avenue, and found a
sleigh waiting before Moyson's boarding house.

" All safe," whispered Jack, " now for a touch of
diplomacy." As he said this he walked up to the
carter who was waiting for Moyson; and after a few
words of conversation I saw the man put something
Jack gave him into his pocket, get up in his seat and
drive off. Jack then gave some instructions to our
carter, and we waited for Moyson's appearance.

He did not keep us long but came running down in
a great hurry, threw a carpet-bag into the sleigh and
was just about jumping in when Jack caught him
roughly by the shoulder and said,

"You're my prisoner!"

He reeled as if he had been struck a heavy blow, and his teeth fairly chattered as he stammered out,

"What do you mean?"

"All right, my tulip," said Jack—it was wonderful to see how naturally Jack played the policeman, that is, the kind of policemen one sees on the stage; "*You* know well enough what I want you for; those flash notes of the Bumptown Bank, you've been shoving lately—it's all right, my beauty, tumble in;" it really was extraordinary how Jack picked up all his slang.

"Who are you, and how dare you stop me?" said Moyson gaining heart a little. "You have no warrant for my arrest."

"Who am I, eh? I am Detective Rocks of the Bumptown force," and he turned back the lappel of his vest and showed a large reporter's badge—for Jack had been a bit of a reporter amongst other things—which Moyson mistook for a detective's shield, "and as for warrants there's half a dozen out for you, here's one if you would like to see it, my buttercup," and he pulled out a large and official looking paper which he flourished before the cashier's eyes; but he never glanced at it, one look at the supposed shield was enough, and he stood perfectly stupefied with fear.

"Now then, look alive, my blooming morning glory" cried Jack pushing him into the sleigh, "we'll make you all comfortable for a few years at government expense, my full blown sunflower." Jack's facility for finding names for him was surprising.

"Wait a minute," cried Moyson as we drove off "I'll give you"—and he whispered something in Jack's ear.

"Will you?" said Jack. "Honor bright."

"Honor bright," replied Moyson, "I've got the money in my pocket."

"All right," said Jack, "we'll have to go to the station, just for form sake, you know, but I'll get you discharged and then you can go."

"How can you get me discharged if I once am in the station?"

"Oh, the easiest thing in the world; when I see you in the light I say I find I have made a mistake in the dark and arrested the wrong man; you come the indignant dodge, threaten to have me dismissed for arresting an innocent citizen and all that sort of thing; nobody there knows you: I admit that I haven't a warrant for your arrest—you not being the man I want and off you go, don't you see!"

"Yes I see it now, all right."

"All right it is," said Jack *sotto voce*. "I'm glad you see it, for if you had resisted I don't know how I should have got you to the station; I suppose it will be all right when I do get you there, although I don't know but what I have made myself amenable to the law for burglary, or something, passing myself off as a detective and arresting a peaceable citizen;

anyhow I'll chance it;" somehow Jack would use
slang even when talking to himself.

It was a funny sight when we reached the station;
there was the French policeman making a charge
against old Dumsic for passing counterfeit money
and resisting the police, for old Dumsic had resisted
considerably as the damaged condition of the policeman's face showed; and there was old Dumsic tearing
and swearing like a wild man, and threatening everybody with destruction if he was not instantly re-
leased. But when the Sergeant ordered old Dumsic
to be searched and two counterfeit ten-dollar bills
were found in his pocket, matters began to look serious, and old Dumsic would probably have been locked
up if Jack and I with Moyson had not happened to
arrive at the time, just as the detective entered with
Thompson and Winnie.

Of course it did not take very long to explain matters to the Sergeant, and Moyson's capture threw an
entirely new light on the subject of Thompson's passing the counterfeit bills; for when he was searched a
large number of counterfeits were found on him, and
seeing there was no chance of escape—for Jack soon
undeceived him about his being a detective—he confessed that he had given the bad bills to Thompson,
and also that when the junior partner had sent to him
for change he had kept the good bill and substituted
another.

It was quite evident that there was no ground for

a charge against Thompson, but as a warrant had been
issued, he had to be taken up to the house of the
magistrate, who, on a representation of the case being
made, accepted bail for his appearance on the day
after Christmas.

Old Dumsie sat on a bench in the Police Station
and abused that French policemen for a good half
hour, which must have been very entertaining to the
man, who did not understand a word of English; and
the man fully explained how the mistake of arresting
him occurred, in French, which was all a mystery to
old Dumsie, who was quite ignorant of that language.
At last old Dumsie got tired of that kind of conversation, and, having deposited a sufficient sum as his
bail to appear and answer the charge of assault, left
the station and went home; but a great change
seemed to have come over him, and he appeared to be
arguing something over to himself as he went along.

I suppose it is scarcely necessary to say that the
Christmas dinner next day was a great success. Of
course Jack was there and had a story all ready to tell
about a friend of his who had got into a scrape very
similar to the one Jack had got into buying his turkey; and very handsome the turkey looked when it
was brought on the table lying helplessly on its back
with its legs in the air; and very merry and jolly we
all prepared to be.

But the funniest thing of all happened just as
Thompson had his knife raised to carve the turkey,

for the door suddenly opened, without any previous warning, and in walked old Dumsie looking a little ashamed of himself I thought, but doing his best to smile pleasantly. He walked right up to Thompson and, offering his hand, said,

"Charlie, I've come to the conclusion that I have been in the wrong, and as I can't prevent your marrying Winnie now, I give my consent. Home don't feel like home at all without Winnie, and I want to have her back. Oh, you shall come too," he continued to Thompson. "I'm going to turn over a new leaf today and what I can't cure, I'm going to endure, and not make myself a fool about it."

Then Winnie looked at Thompson, and Thompson nodded his head, and she tripped up to her father and gave him a sounding kiss, and Thompson shook hands with him and made him sit down to dinner, and the very first cut of the turkey was given to old Dumsie.

It was quite wonderful to see how old Dumsie thawed, just as quick as an icecream pyramid when a red hot poker is applied to it; and awfully jolly he got too, and he and Jack told stories that kept everybody laughing, and old Dumsie had ordered a basket of wine in, and I am afraid Jack and he drank rather too much, for they vowed eternal friendship after all the others had left the table; and Dumsie told Jack he didn't believe he was the descendant of an Irish king at all, and that he would not be at all surprised if his name had originally been Drumstick as Thompson

D

said, and that a very jolly old Drumstick he felt, which everybody knows Dumsic would never have done if he had been quite sober. And the fun we had after the friends who had been invited for the evening arrived, was too much for me to tell, and there was old Dumsic running about making love to all the girls, and declaring he wanted to get married again.

That was last Christmas, and I am going to dine with Thompson again this year, but he doesn't live in "queer quarters" now, but with old Dumsic, who has given him an interest in the pin-and-needle business; and there is to be something more than a Christmas party for there is to be a christening too, and the young gentleman's name is to be Phil after his godfather, and Dumsic after his grandfather, so I will finish my story by wishing long life and happiness to Philip Dumsic Thompson, Esq.

The Christmas Anthem.

THE CHRISTMAS ANTHEM.

It was Christmas Eve, and there was a bustle of preparation for the morrow prevading the little villarge of Goschen, in the Eastern Townships, which gave an appearance of peculiar animation to that usually quiet and staid little place.

In the main street the shops were all aglow with light, and gay parties were hurrying about from shop to shop, some providing for to-morrow's dinner, others engaged in searching for some suitable gift for a friend or relation, and others just strolling idly about to see what their neighbors were doing.

Almost at the head of the main street, standing back some twenty or thirty yards from the highway, in the middle of a small grass plot, which was now covered with snow, was the village church. It was a plain unpretentious edifice of stone, with a steep roof without any tower, belfry or ornament of any kind to set it off. The windows were narrow and of common glass, even the one over the altar was square and of the same plain material. Everything about the place was of the plainest and most rigid character; and the interior had little more ornamentation than the exterior. The pulpit and reading desk were of maple, but simply, almost austerely made, and the altar rails were not even turned, but cut uncompromisingly square.

The only spot which seemed to have escaped the prevailing plainness was the place set apart for the choir, and which boasted nearly all the decoration there was about the church. It stood on the left of the aisle against the wall, not facing the pulpit but at right angles with it, and was raised on a platform about two feet high. This platform projected on three sides beyond the wooden railing and afforded room for a good wide seat, and here strangers were generally accommodated, as the church was small and all the seats taken. There was a harmonium, time-honored and asthmatic, but considered quite a fine instrument in Goschen, and the railing was neatly turned and the wide seat comfortably cushioned, which gave the "music gallery"—as it was ostentatiously termed —a greater air of finish and completeness than any other part of the church, and made it look quite grand in comparison with the surrounding plainness.

The little church was busy and gay this Christmas Eve, like all the rest of Goschen, for the members of the choir had met to practice the Christmas anthem for the last time, and also to decorate the church as far as possible with evergreens and firs.

The practising was over and the Minister's wife, who acted as—what shall I say, organist? she was called the organist in Goschen, but I do not think the title quite correct—sat at the harmonium trying over softly a new and ambitious "voluntary" with which she intended to "play the congregation out" on the next day.

Groups of girls were busying themselves in various parts of the church, twining wreaths around the iron brackets which supported the oil lamps, sticking sprigs of green into the backs of the seats, trying to coax some garlands to hang gracefully about the plain angular reading desk, and otherwise endeavouring to beautify the place and give it an appearance of more cheerfulness than it usually possessed.

Of course there were various young men helping the young ladies—it would be slow work for the young ladies decorating a church if there were no young men to assist them—and most of the young people were gathered in the body of the church chatting gaily and decorating the backs of the seats. A party of three, one lady, two gentlemen, were, with the aid of a ladder, trying to nail to the wall over the altar some letters made of evergreens which were to read,

"Peace on earth, good-will toward men."

Seated in front of the altar rails was a young girl of about twenty, engaged in twisting some wreaths of ever greens about the square rails. She worked in a dull, uninterested way as if she took little pleasure in her task, and at length rested her head on the top of the rail and tears started to her eyes and trickled down her cheeks. She had sat for several minutes this way, with her face buried in her hands, when a hurried step advanced along the chancel and a young man rapidly approaching laid his hand on her shoulder and said gaily,

"Why, Jessie, are you playing hide and seek? I have been looking for you everywhere." Then, as she looked up at him and he saw her tear-stained cheeks, he added in a lower and more tender tone, "Why, you have been crying; what is the matter?"

"Nothing very serious, Bill," answered the girl glancing up at him again, "I have only got a fit of the blues at the thought of how soon I must leave Goschen."

"Leave Goschen!"

"Yes, Bill," she replied sadly, rising and turning away from the altar rail, "leave Goschen, perhaps never to return."

She said no more but walked slowly along the aisle to the choir and seated herself on the broad seat in front of it. The clergyman's wife had finished the "voluntary" and this part of the church was quite deserted. Her companion followed and silently seated himself beside her. After a few moments he asked:

"What do you mean by leaving Goschen, Jessie; is it a joke?"

"If it was it would be a sad one, Bill, but it is only too true. I leave the day after to-morrow."

"But what does it mean?"

"It means, Bill, that sad trouble has come on us, and all Goschen will know it before the year is out. Father is ruined, the farm will have to be sold, and God only knows whether there will be enough left to keep father and mother in their old days. As for me I must work for my living. I have got a situation as companion to a lady in Montreal, and I am to go to her to-morrow."

"Sell Brookside—Squire Barton ruined—you going away—I can't understand it," said Bill, in a puzzled sort of way.

"It is only too true. You see it happened in this way. About two years ago father went security for a friend in Quebec who was entering on a speculation. Mother opposed it but father had great confidence in his friend, who was an old schoolmate, and went his surety. Well, the speculation failed and father had to pay a large sum of money, so large that he didn't have enough, and so the farm had to be mortgaged for $2,000. It was done very quietly in Montreal, and no one knew anything about it. The mortgage was to run for several years if the interest was paid; but you know how everything has gone against father this year, the crops being poor, the stock dying, and then that dreadful fire which destroyed the barn and all it contained. It seemed as if everything was against father and he could not pay the interest, so the lawyers did something or other about it and the farm is to be sold. Of course, there will be something left, for Brookside is worth more than $2,000; but I am afraid it will scarcely be enough to keep father and mother, and I must work for my living."

Mr. William Hayes, who has hitherto been style only "Bill," sat in deep thought for several minutes, then he said,

"Is there no one, Jessie, that your father could apply to for help, no friend, no relative?"

"No," she said, shaking her head sadly, "no one; he has few friends, none who could help him; and as for relatives, I don't think he has one in the world. I never heard of but one, Uncle Robert, and he had a terrible quarrel with father years before I was born before father was married in fact, and he went away and died in Australia. This was before father came to Goschen to live."

"It's awful hard," said Mr. Hayes, scratching his head meditatively as if trying to dig up an idea, "awful hard. But I say," he suddenly added with energy, "if you go away, who is to lead the choir?"

"Nellie Chadworth; I shall sing my last anthem to-morrow. I shall take away many pleasant memories of the choir, and shall often think of the old church, and the many happy hours I have spent in it, when I am far away."

The tears started to her eyes again and she turned aside to hide her emotion.

Mr. William Hayes, bachelor, aged twenty-five, good looking and in excellent physical health, sat drumming with his heels against the seat, firmly believing he was the most miserable man in existence. He had grown up from childhood with Jessie Barton, and his love for her had become part of his very life. There was no formal engagement, no vows of love had ever passed between them, but everyone looked upon it as a settled thing, that Bill Hayes was to marry Jessie Barton sometime—when his father died, most people said. Mr. Hayes sat drumming with his heels, and bitterly thought of what he was, and what was his position. Now was the time when he ought to tell her about his love and offer to guard and protect her; but, how was he to do it? What was he? Nothing! Simply a hanger-on upon his father: a clerk in his store in the village, and receiving the munificent salary of $400 a year and his board, and lodging. This supported him well as a bachelor in a quiet country village like Goschen, but how could he support a wife and prospective family on it? Certainly his father was rich, by far the richest man in Goschen, and he was his only child; but Bill knew his father well, a hard, stern, cold, grasping man who would never consent to his only son's marriage to a poor portionless girl; and who would, in all probability disinherit that son if he dared to disobey him or thwart his wishes. And so Mr. Hayes sat and drummed away, thinking what a fool he had been not to have gone to California four years ago, when his cousin Tom Reeves went. Tom had made quite a little fortune in that time and wrote home, giving glowing accounts of his success.

While Mr. Hayes drummed away and mentally called himself any quantity of hard names, Jessie still sat with her head averted, and the tears coursing silently down her cheeks. It is a dangerous position for a man madly in love, to find himself seated by the object of his affection, and to see her in tears. Mr Hayes resisted as long as possible, but his love was too strong for his determination, and suddenly, he scarce knew how, he found his arm around Jessie' waist, and as he drew her to him, he whispered passionately:

"Jessie, darling, I know I am a great fool; I know I am not worthy of you; but I love you"—

"There, there, let us go!" exclaimed Jessie, rising suddenly with glowing cheeks; "they are putting out the lights, and we shall be locked in."

So saying she walked down the aisle, followed by Mr. Hayes, who felt more convinced than ever that he was a fool.

* * * * * *

"It is just what Christmas ought to be." That was what Farmer Bulrush said next morning, and Farmer Bulrush was an authority upon the weather for ten miles around Goshen, and certainly ought to have known what he was talking about. Certain it was that the day was clear, cold and bright, with the thermometer about 15° below freezing, and just enough sun to make a sharp walk pleasant. Everybody and everything looked gay and bright in the sunshine, and I rather incline to Farmer Bulrush's opinion that it was "just what Christmas ought to be."

The bell in the little church had not ceased ringing, for the very good and sufficient reason that it had never begun; in fact, there was no bell at all, but the congregation had assembled in full force, and the building was crowded to its utmost capacity.

Jessie sat in her accustomed place as leader of the choir, and the paleness of her countenance, and the half mournful manner in which she looked about the church from time to time, as if taking leave of some familiar object, showed how much she felt and grieved at the fact that she sat in her accustomed place for, perhaps, the last time.

The service was pretty well advanced when a stranger entered the church. He did not seem at first as if he intended to enter, for, after he had put his head in he withdrew it for a moment; but, muttering, "I can rest here as well as anywhere else," advanced a little way up the aisle. In a moment the sexton saw him, and pouncing on him carried him off in triumph to the strangers' seat, where he was placed in the corner next to Jessie. The sexton obsequiously handed him a book, but he opened it mechanically, without looking at the page, and seemed to take little interest in the service.

He was a curious looking man, this stranger, old,

with scanty white locks and crows' feet deep around his eyes. Yet, it did not seem to be age alone which had blanched his hair and lined his face, for his form was erect and strong, and the bright flash of his eye told of health and vigor yet. He looked rather like a man whose hair had been prematurely whitened by care and sorrow, than one who was far on in the vale of years.

He glanced about him from time to time, and a half smile curled his lips as the solemn words of the Litany fell upon his ear, and he muttered to himself, "all nonsense; all nonsense."

Suddenly there was a pause; the congregation rose from their knees, and the clergyman gave out the anthem. It was not exactly an anthem, it was one of the hymns for Christmas day, but it had been carefully practised for weeks, and arranged so that the soprano should sing one verse, the tenor the next, and "everybody" join in the chorus, and great things were expected of it.

The wheezy little harmonium sighed out the overture, there was a slight pause, the rustling of dresses as the congregation rose, and then a clear, sweet, full young voice, pure and musical as the song of some joyous bird, burst forth in the full tide of melody with the glorious old Christmas hymn,

>"Hark! the herald angels sing,
>"Glory to the new-born King,
>"Peace on earth and mercy mild,
>"God and sinners reconcil'd."

Grandly, the full, round voice rose to the majestic melody of the hymn, and the whole building seemed to echo again and again with the glad tidings that Christ was born to save sinners.

When the sound fell on his ear, the old man turned and looked long and earnestly at the fair singer. Jessie Barton was not what would be called a pretty girl; her features were not regular, but her complexion was fair, and her face pure and good; and as she stood now, her bright blue eyes sparkling with animation, her light golden hair streaming unbound over her shoulders, her cheeks slightly flushed, and her whole soul seemingly absorbed in singing her Creator's praise, she looked almost beautiful.

The old man put his hand to his ear and sat quietly listening, and long after the hymn was finished he kept repeating to himself,

"Peace on earth and mercy mild,
"God and sinners reconcil'd."

Then he would look over the altar, and read the words,

"Peace on earth, good will toward men,"

And he would shake his head and mutter, "I can't understand it; it used to be all hell-fire and damnation in my day, but it's changed now. I should like to ask her about it," and he turned and looked again at the calm, pure face beside him. The old man's attention never wandered from the service again, and he listened

meekly and reverently to the sermon, as if trying
to reconcile it in his mind with something he had
heard before ; but he still sat with his head turned a
little on one side and his hand to his ear, while he
gazed quietly, but not impertinently at the calm
face of Jessie Barton.

It wasn't a brilliant sermon ; it was simply a re-
count of the plan of salvation, and a brief history of
the Nativity of the Saviour ; but the preacher was
earnest and impressive, and carried a conviction
of the Creator's love and tenderness home to the
hearts of his hearers, as he dwelt on the love and
mercy of the Omnipotent, and entreated them to
trust to Him, to cast their sins and sorrows upon Him,
and to avail themselves of the way provided by Him
for them to escape the wages of sin ; and still the old
man listened and occasionally murmured, " I should
like to ask her about it."

The service was over, and the congregation had all
dispersed ; Jessie was almost the last person to leave
the church, for she lingered to say good-bye to her
friends, and after that, was busied in packing up her
music to take home with her for the last time.

As she passed out of the door, after shaking hands
with the sexton and bidding him good-bye, a man,
who had evidently been waiting for her, came up and
quietly walked by her side. She looked up and saw
the old man who had sat by her in church. He did not
look like a beggar, he was well dressed and seemed

warm and comfortable; his clothes, although not exactly new, were of good quality and well made, and he walked erect, with his head up and an elastic, independent stride like a man who owed the world nothing and asked no favors of it. He walked on for a few yards in silence and then said, abruptly,

"Do you believe it?"

"Believe what?" asked Jessie. She was surprised, but not the least bit frightened at the old man's conduct, for it was broad daylight and she was within a hundred yards of her father's house, and some of the congregation were only a short distance ahead of her.

"What you were singing just now,

Peace on earth and mercy mild,
God and sinners reconcil'd."

and he was preaching about Christ dying to save sinners—do you believe it?"

"Do I believe the story of the Saviour offering himself a sacrifice for our sins? Of course I do! Don't you?"

"I don't know, it seems so strange. I haven't been in a church for nigh on twenty years, and then they used to preach about hell-fire and damnation; it all seems so strange." He walked on quietly by her side for some time without saying any more, until Jessie stopped before a comfortable looking farm-house, then he asked; "Would you mind talking it over with an old man?"

Jessie hesitated and then said,

"You had better talk to the minister, sir, he is so much wiser, and knows so much better than me."

"No. It was your voice roused me, not his; I'd rather talk to you."

"Jessie," called her mother coming to the door, "why don't you come in, dinner's waiting on the table?'

Jessie looked from the old man to her mother and seemed in doubt what to do; at last she asked the old man to "wait a minute," and going to her mother said,

"Mother, here is an old gentleman who was at church and walked home with me, asking me such queer questions, and he says he wants to talk with me. What shall I do?"

"Well, child," her mother replied, "you know your father's notions about Christmas; he would'nt let a dog go from his door on a Christmas Day. Ask the gentleman in to dinner and you can talk to him after; the turkey is small, but it will be enough."

Jessie did as she was bid. At first the old man would not hear of it, and insisted upon going to the inn and returning after dinner; but Jessie finally persuaded him and he went in.

"Father, this gentleman is a stranger in the village, he says he would like to talk to me about something; and I have asked him to dine with us."

"Quite right, Jessie," said Mr. Barton rising and advancing toward the stranger, with outstretched hand. "You are heartily welcome, Sir," he continued addressing his guest, "our fare is plain, but what there is I shall be happy to have you with us to share. I have some queer notions, folks tell me, about Christmas, and I never allow any stranger to pass my door on that day; if there is nothing else to offer there is a hearty welcome, and I take it that's worth something. So come right in, Sir, dinner's on the table, and the wife will fret if we let it get cold."

Mr. Barton was a hale, hearty specimen of a farmer; tall, broad-chested, bronzed with exposure, his hand hard with honest labor, and the frost of over fifty winters just showing itself through his dark locks. His face was soft and kindly, and a pleasant sort of smile was fond of playing about the corners of his mouth. Take him for all in all one would be apt to say on seeing him, "that is an honest man."

The dinner passed off merrily; the old gentleman developed a fund of wit which no one had expected of him, and seemed to be well informed on every subject. He had travelled a great deal, had been whaling in the Arctic Seas, and hunting tigers in Central Africa; he had been amongst the pearl divers in the Indian Ocean, and had mined in California and Nevada. Many strange stories and amusing anecdotes he told, and kept his audience fully amused during the meal.

After dinner they went into the parlor, and while Mr. Barton took his usual nap, Jessie opened the piano and sung some of her favorite hymns for the old man.

"Thank you, my dear," he said, when she had finished. "And now I want to ask you a question; you have treated an old man and a stranger very kindly, and he does not even know who to thank. What is your name?"

"Jessie Barton."

"Barton, Barton!" he exclaimed in some surprise. "Any relation to the Bartons who used to live in Sherbrooke many years ago?"

"We are the same family, sir. I was born in Sherbrooke, father moved to Goschen years ago."

The old man bowed his head in his hands for a minute and said softly to himself, "I believe it now,

"Peace on earth, good will toward men."

Just then the farmer stirred in his sleep and waking with a sudden snort looked about him, and tried very hard to pretend he had never been asleep at all.

The old man rose and crossing to him said, very solemnly:

"Alfred Barton, do you remember thirty years ago quarrelling with your brother in the old homestead in Sherbrooke?"

"Aye, aye, Bob was always a hasty lad; but he had a good heart."

"Do you remember how he cursed you, and swore he would never break bread with you, or recognize you as a brother again?"

"Aye, aye, but I know he was sorry for it afterwards ; and if he had lived I believe he would have come back years ago and told me so."

"He does live; he has come back; he is sorry for it," exclaimed the old gentleman in excited tones. "Good God, Alfred, is it possible we have both changed so much in thirty years that we cannot recognize each other ?"

The two men looked into each other's faces for nearly a minute, then their hands met with a hearty grip, and two words escaped them.

"Robert !"

"Alfred !"

And so the quarrel of thirty years ago was made up.

After a while the farmer spoke, still holding his brother's hand :

"Robert, lad, you've come back at a bad time ; the farm is about to be sold, and there will not be much left; but much or little, we'll share it together, lad, for so I know the father would have wished, although he said nothing about it in the will, thinking you were dead."

"And so you'll share with me," said the old man, a tear beginning to creep into the corner of his eye.

"Aye, lad, there's not much ; but there's a hearty welcome."

"And I'll share with you," said the old man, bringing his hand down with a jolly smack into the farmer's right hand which he had seized and turned palm upwards all ready to be smacked. "I'll share with you and you won't get the worst of the bargain, for the rolling stone has gathered some moss this time, and Robert Barton is good for a quarter of a million any time. Yes," he continued after a pause, "I am a rich man, Alfred, but a very lonely, solitary one. I have never known what it was to have a home since I left the old place; no wife, no children, I stand all alone in my old days; let me end them with you; let us old men try to bring back some of our boyhood's days; let your daughter be my daughter, and let us spend what little of life is left us, together. I have done enough for riches, let me do something for happiness."

My story is as good as finished; Brookside was not sold, and Jessie did not go to Montreal. Mr. Hayes, somehow, found courage to finish that little speech he commenced in the church, and Jessie did not interrupt him; and when his father found he was going to marry a rich heiress instead of a penniless girl, he gave him a splendid house and made over the business to him.

There is a little "Bill," and a little "Jessie," and a little "Bob" now, and Jessie looks quite matronly although she still leads the choir; and the old man sits in the strangers' seat—he will take no other—and listens to her pure voice, and says that he never began to feel what true happiness meant, until he heard that Christmas anthem:

"Peace on earth and mercy mild,
"God and sinners reconcil'd."

The Policeman's Christmas.

THE POLICEMAN'S CHRISTMAS.

BY ONE OF THE FORCE.

Perhaps you are one of the people who don't think a policeman ought to want to keep Christmas like other folks; maybe you belong to that class who believe that a policeman ought always to be "on his beat," and that he should never fail to be just on the very spot in that beat—no matter if it be two or three miles long, as it often is—at the very moment that a burglary is being committed, or a fire breaks out, or a child gets run over, or a fight takes place, or a drunken man slips on the sidewalk, or any other accident occurs. Possibly you think, like a great many do, that a policeman hasn't got the same feelings as other people, that, when he puts on his blue coat with brass buttons and sticks his staff in his belt he ceases to be an ordinary man and becomes "a limb of the law," something of a nondescript animal, half man, half locust club. Don't you believe anything of the kind. Long service, getting used to rough life and mixing with the lowest classes; seeing human-nature it its worst and always having to keep a bright lookout for others' failings, don't tend to elevate a man; I admit that; it isn't the sort of work that tends to improve a man's opinion of humanity; it's not the sort of thing to make a man think better of his fellow men; still, I don't believe you can ever make a policeman quite a machine like we are told a soldier can be made—though I have my doubts about that, too.

You see we have to mix too much with the people to get all the man taken out of us and leave nothing but the machine, doing its duty and knowing or caring nothing beyond. It isn't natural to suppose that we can be on the force for any length of time without making a good many acquaintances, and, perhaps, a few friends. We are for the most part pretty nearly always on the same beats; of course, we are changed about every now and then so that we may get well acquainted with the city, but we keep pretty well to one station, and get to know most of the people we meet. It isn't always that we know them to speak to, but just by sight, and many a time on a cold, raw, winter's morning, it has given me a sort of comfortable feel to meet some great gentleman I know by sight, and to feel that the wind and the snow, and the cold didn't have any more respect for him than it did for the poor policeman who was nearly dead with the three hours' freezing he had got on his beat.

When I say, "got acquainted," I don't mean in the way you read in thrashy novels—written by people who know nothing of the force—about policemen, being always dodging down area ways to spark

cooks, and arresting small boys, and never being on
their beats when wanted, and running away when
they hear a row; that's for the most part all stuff
written by people who don't know what they are
writing about. I ask you as a sensible person—I
suppose you are a sensible person, tho' I may be mistaken,—did you ever see a policeman hanging about
area railings making love to the cook or the house
maid, either for her own sake, or for the sake of the
broken victuals? Did you ever see a policeman
arrest a small boy, except those nuisances who will
go coasting down steep streets when there's any
snow, to the great danger of their own necks and of
damage to all passers-by—that sort have to be arrested
once in a while just to frighten the rest a bit; but did
you ever know a policeman who made it a practice
of arresting only small boys? I'll bet you never did,
and never saw one except on the stage, or in a comic
paper. And as for running away from rows—well,
if you're green enough to believe that, I'm sorry for
you, that's all. No, the sort of acquaintances I mean
that a policeman makes is mostly the people he
passes and repasses on the street and the people he
has to arrest.

Were you ever arrested? Well, you needn't get
mad at the question, quite as good men as you have
been arrested, and it don't always prove, because a
man is arrested that he has done anything wrong;
but if you ever should be arrested it might, perhaps,
surprise you to find yourself known by some one or

more of the force, if not by name at least by sight, altho'
you are a very quiet, respectable citizen, " unknown
to the police," as the saying is. You might not know
a single policeman by sight, but the chances are that
some of them know you ; why, Lor' bless me ! put the
police force of Montreal, small as it is, in the middle
of the Champ the Mars, and let all the grown up men
and women—and a good show of the children too—
pass round them, and I'll bet my buttons, and that's
a good deal for a policeman to bet, that at least a
quarter of them could be recognized by some member
of the force. You see it's sort of natural—at least it
is to me, and I suppose it is to most of the force—to
look pretty sharp about us as we go up and down our
beats, and from meeting the same people frequently
and forming acquaintances with the shop-keepers and
such like, who are generally very glad to be acquainted with " the policeman on the beat,"—we get
to know pretty nearly everybody who passes along
our beat every day or so.

I remember when I first went to the Ottawa Street
Station, I was quite a stranger to that part of the
city, and knew very little about Griffintown except that
it had a bad name, and I didn't feel as if my life was
quite safe there at first, but, bless you, a name is all
in this world. " Give a dog a bad name and hang
him," you know the old saying; Griffintown isn't
really much worse than many other localities where
the poor live, but it's got the name and it will stick

to it. I used to keep my eye pretty well open, and I soon had to make a good many arrests for drunkenness and corner loafing. Corner loafing is the besetting sin of the youth of Griffintown. Whenever a young fellow can beg, borrow, or steal the time from himself or anybody else, he thinks it the proper thing to "hang on" at one of the corners, Kempt and Ottawa is the most fashionable corner, but Colborne, McCord and other streets get a good share of patronage.

About the first man I arrested was a young fellow who went by the nickname of "Rowdy Ducks," and who had the reputation of being one of the "hardest" cases in Griffintown; his right name was Roderick Duckworth, but he was best known to the police by the *sobriquet* his misconduct had earned for him. He was drunk when I arrested him, and resisted a bit so that I had great trouble in getting him to the station; but I managed it at last, and next morning, he having been up very often of late, the Recorder sent him down for two months.

Rowdy's friends told me to "look out" for myself when he came out, as he never forgot or forgave a policeman who had once arrested him; but I soon found I had nothing to fear, and after a little we got to be quite friendly, and he used to come up to my house some nights when I was off duty to smoke a friendly pipe. He was quite a decent young fellow as long as he would leave drink alone, and quite intelligent. He was a plumber by trade, and a first-rate workman, so that he never wanted long for a job.

He got a little steadier that summer, and was only arrested two or three times for drunkenness, but as he had money he paid his fine and was not sent down.

A couple of nights after his last arrest I was off duty, and he came up to my house, so I took the opportunity of talking to him a bit.

"Look here, Rowdy," I said,—we generally called him Rowdy,—"what is the good of your going on this way; you're a young man and a good workman, and you ought to be ashamed of yourself to go to the dogs the way you are going now; why don't you marry and settle down?"

He flushed up a little when I said this, and tried to laugh it off; but after a while he said, quite serious like:

"I've thought about it Barnes," (my name is Barnes —S. C. Barnes—S. C. stands for Samuel Charles, not Sub Constable, although I am one) "but I don't know exactly how it would do. You see the devil seems to get into me when I have a drop of drink, and I don't know what I am doing. I am half afraid to trust myself, for I should hate myself if I married Mollie and then abused her as I see some men do."

"Oh, ho!" I said, "it's gone as far as that has it; well, Roddy, my man, take a fool's advice, swear off drink, marry Mollie, and settle down for a while out of Griffintown, where you will be away from your old companions and out of the way of temptation. You ought to be too much of a man to let drink get the best of you at your age; if you don't put your foot down like a man and kill your taste for it now, you won't be able to do it in ten years time, if you live so long."

"Well, old man," he answered, "I'll think about it: I've got a good place now, and this would be about as good a time as any for me to turn over a new leaf; perhaps, I'll do it. Good night, old man."

"Good night, my boy, and stick to your good resolution."

I lost sight of Roddy for some time after that, and the winter was nearly gone when I met him again. It was one morning when I was one of the first relief, and had the Wellington Street beat; perhaps, I had better explain here how the men are divided at the stations, as you may possibly understand my story better then.

Every policeman is on duty for twelve hours during one half of the month, and sixteen hours a day for the other half—how is that for work, you eight and nine hour men who grumble at what you have to do, and talk about " the lazy police?" The day men have to be at the station at six o'clock in the morning, and are then divided into two reliefs, first and second; the first relief goes on duty on the beats from six o'clock until nine, and are then relieved, going on patrol again at twelve o'clock for three hours more;

both reliefs remain on duty—either on the boats or at the station—until six o'clock in the evening. The night duty men have to report at the station at two o'clock in the afternoon—except those who make prisoners the night before and have to attend the Recorder's Court, they are generally allowed until five o'clock to report—and remain on duty until six next morning. That is pretty good time it seems to me, and the pay was only a dollar a day t. en—it's been raised to eight dollars a week now for ⟨ ⟩ hands, and little enough it is at that I say. The night men have to report in the afternoon because they have to do odd jobs, notifying persons who have committed a breach of any of the Corporation By-laws, by keeping dogs without paying the tax and such like matters. Every two weeks the day men become the night men, so that we change and change about.

I think that is enough explanation for the present, so I'll get back to my story. I was on the first relief of the day duty men, and just as I walked down Wellington Street, I saw Roddy crossing the bridge—this was before the present railway bridge was built—coming from Point St. Charles way. He was looking better than I ever saw him look before, neat and tidy, and his clothes all nicely brushed, and altogether quite smartened up from what he used to be. He saw me about as quick as I saw him and came across the street, laughing and holding his hand out;

"Well, old man," he said as soon as we had shaken

hands, "
little girl
and I'm
" That
didn't lik
changed
more hea
and who
Montreal
" I'm r
" but I h
own and
look ahe
know."
It was
moment,
father of
" Well,
chickens
like looki
spoke to
" Yes,
" Well,
I shall be
glad to k
" That
walked o
You se
ceremony

hands, "I've taken your advice. I've got as nice a little girl as you could find in a day's travel, for a wife, and I'm living out at the Point and keeping steady."

"That's right, Duckworth," I said—somehow I didn't like to call him "Rowdy" now he was so much changed for the better, "nobody congratulates you more heartily than I do; stick to your new way of life, and who knows but what you may be Mayor of Montreal one of these days."

"I'm not such a fool as to expect that," replied he, "but I hope in a couple of years to start a shop of my own and begin business on my own hook. I've got to look ahead now a little more than I used to, you know."

It was astonishing how paternal he looked at that moment, anybody might have thought he was the father of a large family.

"Well," I said, laughing, "you are counting your chickens before they are hatched, but there is nothing like looking ahead. And who is the wife, the one you spoke to me about?"

"Yes. I'd like you to see her, Barnes."

"Well, just you bring her up next Sunday evening; I shall be off duty at six, and my old woman will be glad to know her."

"That I will, and thank you too," he said, and walked off to his business.

You see we poor people can't afford to stand on ceremony like rich folks; there's no need of calling

F

cards, and previous introductions, and formal invitations with us; if we want a man to come and see us we ask him right off, and if he wants to come, he comes; and if he don't want to come he stays away, that's all.

Roddy came on the Sunday night, and brought his wife. She was a very pretty girl, was Mollie Duckworth, almost too pretty I thought, and seemed very fond of Roddy; but somehow, I can't say, I took a fancy to her, and my old woman didn't like her at all.

"She's a wild, flirting thing, that cares for nothing but dress and nonsense," said my old woman after they were gone, "and is no fit wife for a working man like Rowdy. Mark my words," she continued, "he'll be sorry for it before a year is out;" having delivered which opinion she marched off to bed.

I used to see Rowdy pretty often that summer going to work in the morning, and two or three times he came to see us, and one Sunday my old woman and I took tea with him at his house. He had been married near a year then and was still living out at the Point, but talked of coming up to the city in the winter, as he said he was too far from his business. His wife seemed anxious for him to come into town too, declaring she was "moped to death" out there, and although I tried to persuade him not to come back to the old place, I could see he had made up his mind, and I felt pretty sure it would not be long before he was in Griffintown again and, perhaps, up to his old games.

They did not seem to get along well together; he
was very fond of her but she appeared careless about
him, and rather free for a married woman; still I
thought that would wear off, the more so as there was
a prospect of there being a little Roddy before very
long. We did not spend a very pleasant evening, and
my old woman would not go again although they
asked us.

Early in the fall they left the Point and came to
live in Barré Street, where they had half of a small
brick house, and Mollie kept house after a fashion;
but most of her time was spent gadding about St.
Joseph Street and around that portion of the city,
instead of minding her duties at home, and I could
see that Roddy was not very comfortable with his
wife. Still he kept steady for a while and did not go
with his old companions; but it did not last long. The
baby was born early in November and died in a few
days, and after that Mollie was out more than ever,
and neglected the house so that Roddy was never quite
certain that he would get anything for supper when
he came home after work.

This soon brought about the result I expected;
finding he could get no comfort at home, Roddy fell
back into his old habits, and one night I found him
loitering, half drunk, at the corner of Kempt and
Ottawa Streets. I did not take him in charge but
walked home with him part of the way, giving him a
bit of advice.

"I can't help it, Barnes," he said, "Mollie is driv[ing] me to it with her careless ways. I never get any peace or comfort in the house, and to-night she nevc[r] came home to get supper; so I went off with the boy[s] a bit and had a few drinks. I haven't been drinkin[g] lately you know, and a little got the best of m[e] Barnes, old fellow," he went on after a minute, " [I] wish I never had married; I don't think Mollie care[s] much about me, and perhaps never did, although [I] have been a good kind husband to her. She likes an[y] place better than her home, and sometimes I think —"—he didn't finish what he thought, but I could hea[r] his teeth grind together in a way that made my fles[h] creep all over and a little cold shiver run right throug[h] me. I never did like to hear people grind their teet[h] but I never heard any teeth get such a grinding a[s] Roddy gave his that night.

"Never mind, old fellow," I said, trying to chee[r] him up a bit, "she's young yet, and when the kid[s] begin to come she will settle down at home neve[r] fear. Are you all right now," I asked as we reache[d] his door, "if so, I'll leave you. Go to bed, Rodd[y] and don't come out again to-night, or you might ge[t] into trouble."

"I'm all right, old man," he said as he opened th[e] door. "Good night."

He went in as he spoke, leaving the door partl[y] open, and I could see Mollie sitting by the tabl[e] reading something which she hastily put in he[r] pocket as she heard Roddy's step in the room. "This is a nice time for you to come home, and a pretty condition you are in," she said, turning on him sharply.

"Where have you been all the afternoon?" he retorted angrily. "Why didn't you come home to get supper?"

I didn't catch any more, but I could hear their voices raised as I walked away, and I knew they were having a row.

After that, Roddy "went to the dogs," as the saying is, faster than ever. He soon was out of work, and spent most of his time loafing at street corners or drinking in the saloons. I saw him drunk several times, but he kept away from me, and as he behaved himself quietly and did not make a row I didn't arrest him, and he managed to keep out of the station house. I knew he and Mollie were getting on worse than ever together, for I heard some of his companions taking about it; but Roddy evidently did not want to speak to me of it, and avoided me as much as possible.

It was two nights before Christmas, and I was resting myself a bit in the station, and thinking whether the old woman would have a turkey or a goose for Christmas dinner, when a boy came running in and said, the police were wanted down in Barré street, that a man had killed his wife there.

It was almost eleven o'clock, and I was pretty well

tired out, having been on duty since two o'clock trying to catch some boys who would insist on coasting down Mountain street, at the imminent risk of their own necks and other people's limbs; and I had also been three hours on patrol, but I jumped up quite fresh and lively the moment the boy spoke, for it flashed across me in a minute that the man was Roddy, so I pulled on my coat and taking another man with me started for Barré street.

The street was all in a bustle when I got there, and quite a crowd had collected in front of Roddy's, from whence sounds of swearing and a smashing like furniture being broken, and a woman's cries and sobs proceeded.

I pushed my way through the crowd into the house and found everything in confusion. Roddy was standing in the middle of the room with the fragment of a chair in his hand which he had been smashing to pieces, his face was terribly flushed, his eyes flashing, and his whole manner showed that he was laboring under great excitement besides being very drunk; Mollie was in one corner with her hands pressed to her head, sobbing and shrieking out, "Murder," every now and then; the furniture was all knocked about, and looked as if there had been a scuffle in the room. The moment Mollie saw me she ran to me and shouted out: "Save me, Mr. Barnes, he tried to kill me!"

"And I will too," growled Roddy savagely, "You won't carry on your games much longer at my ex-

pense, my girl," and he took a step towards her with
the piece of broken chair raised above his head, but
stopped ashamed like when he saw me.

"It's all right, old man," he said, trying to laugh:
"I was only making fun, I wouldn't hurt her."

"He struck me," cried Mollie, "see here," and she
took her hand from her face and showed me a great
red mark on one side which looked as if she had been
struck with an open hand. "He struck me twice
and swore he'd kill me, and I want him arrested. I'm
afraid to trust myself with him. Take him away and
lock him up."

"I only gave her a slap, Barnes," said Roddy. "I'm
a little drunk and she made me mad; it's all right
now, I won't touch her again."

He spoke quite rationally although he was drunk,
and his passion was all gone, so I talked the matter
over a little with him and quieted him down before I
took him to the station, for I could not help arresting
him as Mollie continued to make her charge against
him. He went very quietly; but I could see he felt being arrested again after keeping out of the station so
long.

It was near twelve o'clock when I got back to the
station, and time for me to go on my beat, so Roddy
was kept a few minutes until the second relief came
in, when some of the men were to take him up to the
Chaboillez Square station where all prisoners from
Ottawa street had to be taken in those days, as there
were no cells in Ottawa street.

"Don't swear too hard against me to-morrow morning, old man," said Roddy as I went out. "I didn't mean to hurt the girl, and it is the first time I ever struck her."

When I came off my beat at three o'clock, I heard that the men who were taking Roddy up to Chaboillez Square, had been set upon by a lot of Roddy's friends at the corner of Colborne and William streets, and a rescue effected; Grigson, one of the officers, had got a bad cut over the eye with a stick, and the other man had been pretty roughly handled. A squad of men had been down to Roddy's house looking for him, but he had not been there. I was sorry Roddy had been rescued, for I knew he would soon be caught again and it would go harder with him then.

Next morning I had to go up to the Recorder's Court about the boys I had been chasing the day before, three of whom we had caught. I was a bit late, for I had overslept myself, and was hurrying along William street when just about Colborne a gentleman stopped me and asked me a question. It was a bitter cold morning and the wind was blowing right through me, so that I didn't hear him at first. It's no use telling me that the wind never blows *through* a man but round him, I know better; I've felt it many a time come in at the third button-hole of my coat, just about the pit of my stomach, bore a straight hole clean through me, and go out at the small of my back. It has happened to me frequently, so I ought

THE POLICEMAN'S CHRISTMAS.   81

to know; any way, this morning the wind had stopped up my ears and I had to ask the gentleman to repeat his question. "Can you tell me the way to Barré street, if you please?"

I gave him the direction, and wondered a bit what a swell like him could want in Barré street. He was a very fancy sort of a fellow with a handsome seal skin coat, cap and gloves on, and very new pants, I could tell they were very new for the basting thread had not been pulled out on one side, and they didn't bulge out at the knees like old pants do. He was a good looking chap too, with bushy black hair and a big moustache, but there was a wicked look about the eyes I didn't like; however, I had not much time to waste, for it was nearly ten, and I hurried off to the court.

The Recorder was on the bench when I got in and the first case had been called; it was a simple drunk, and soon disposed off, then the Recorder astonished me by calling out "Roderick Duckworth!"

I was thoroughly surprised for I did not know he had been re-arrested, and I hastily arose to go into the box, thinking it was my case.

"Why, it's Rowdy!" exclaimed His Honor, a smile of recognition playing over his good humored countenance as the prisoner stepped into the dock, "so you've come back again Rowdy, eh?"

"My name isn't Rowdy," said Roddy sulkily.

"The more reason for you to be ashamed that your

misconduct has gained such a *sobriquet* for you," returned His Honor, taking him up quite sharp. "What is the charge?"

The officers who arrested him stated that he had been found in St. Charles Borroméo Street about three o'clock in the morning very drunk, and taken to the Central Station, where it was discovered that he had been arrested in Griffintown and subsequently rescued.

"What was he arrested for, the first time?" asked His Honor.

"He was drunk in his own house, your Honor," replied the Sergeant, "and beat his wife."

"Oh," said His Honor, looking crossly at Roddy, "you have added that to your other accomplishments, have you. Well, go on with the case; has the woman made a charge against him?"

There was a pause for an instant and I saw Roddy look up and throw an anxious, inquiring glance around the Court to see if Mollie was there. Not finding her his face cleared, but it clouded over again in an instant as he saw the Clerk of the Court enter with a sheet of paper in his hand, closely followed by Mollie who had a handkerchief ostentatiously tied across her face covering her left eye.

His Honor read the deposition and putting on his sternest look, said, "Duckworth, you are charged with committing a violent assault on your wife, by striking her with your fist in the face inflicting a severe wound. There is no class of men," continued His Honor, settling himself down for a little lecture, "whom I more cordially abhor than the mean, cowardly wretches who raise their hands against weak, defenseless women; there is nothing more cowardly, nothing more ruffianly than the wife-beater, and I often regret that the law does not allow me to condemn them to a number of lashes with the cat-o'-nine tails, so that they may feel some of that corporal suffering they are so fond of inflicting upon others. You have long been known to this Court as a drunken loafer, and now you have added another crime to the long list already against you, one too, of the worst crimes a man can be guilty of. Here is a young, delicate woman—scarcely more than a girl—whom you have sworn before God's holy altar to cherish and protect, and I find you using brutal violence towards her, such as no man with any feeling would use to a dog. I warn you, sir, that the Court will not be disposed to be any too lenient to you, and unless you amend your way of living, your course will lead you down to—to—perdition," concluded His Honor, rather bothered for a moment for a word; but getting it, started off again. "Yes, to perdition, and, perhaps, will lead you to the gallows, for in a moment of drunken delirium, when your unbridled passions are allowed full sway, you may strike the blow which will place you in the murderer's cell." Having thus comfortably disposed of Roddy, His Honor asked for the evidence and ordered Mollie to be sworn.

"Your Honor," said Roddy, earnestly, "I never raised my hand against her before, and she drove me to it with her flirting ways. I haven't been here for eighteen months, and I would never have come here again but for her."

"That will do, that will do; you will have an opportunity to say what you have to say by and by. Go on with the evidence."

Mollie took her place in the witness-box, and after darting a vindictive glance at Roddy gave her evidence. It was dead against Roddy, and showed him as a regular ruffian who continually illused her, and who had walked into the house and without a word of provocation felled her to the ground, giving her, as she expressed it, "an awful cut" on the forehead.

"Poor thing," said His Honor, very compassionately, "it is a mercy he did not kill you in his brutality. Take off the bandage, if you can, and let me see the wound."

"I only struck her with the back of my hand, your Honor," put in Roddy, "it would not have killed a fly."

"Hold your tongue, sir; you have no legal right to strike her at all. Let me see the injury."

Mollie coquetted a good deal about taking off the handkerchief and began to cry, and said it hurt her too much and a lot more stuff, so His Honor kindly told her not to mind, and Mollie brightened up in a moment and shot a glance of triumph at Roddy; but

I wasn't going to see him beaten that way, so I just slipped my thumb under the knot of the handkerchief, gave a pull and brought it away, very nearly pulling off her bonnet in the operation.

His Honor looked for a moment as if he was going to read me a lecture for my officiousness, but his attention was distracted by a suppressed cry from Mollie and he turned to her, so I escaped.

She had flushed up as red as a beet, and looked at me as if she would like to bite me, but I didn't mind that; I was watching His Honor who was looking at her face.

There was not a mark or a scratch on it.

His Honor gazed at her steadily for a moment and a sterner look came over his face. He has a keen sense of humor has His Honor, and I have often seen him laugh at his own jokes; but he has also a keen sense of justice, and an honest, kindly heart beats beneath his judicial waistcoat. Mollie saw that she had gone too far and stammered out:

"He didn't cut me, your Honor, he stunned me and it hurt awfully."

"Is that the only *mark* you have got?"

Mollie nodded assent, and His Honor continued, "it doesn't seem to be a very dangerous wound; let me hear what the policeman has to say."

My evidence was soon given as well as that of the officer who accompanied me. His Honor paused for a moment, and then asked the Sergeant on duty how long it was since Roddy had been before him.

The Sergeant referred to the book and said it was eighteen months, and I took the chance to put in a good word for him.

"Duckworth," said His Honor, "I find that the charge against you does not seem to be so grave as it appeared at first; your wife's statement is rather vague, and seems to be dictated to some extent by spite, and is not borne out by the policeman's statement. I am glad to hear you have been more steady of late, and hope you will let this be a warning to you not to fall back into your old evil courses. It is really a pity that you and your wife cannot get on more comfortably together, you are both young and should try to live happily together. I shall give you a chance this time; but, mind, if you are brought before me again for the same offense I shall send you down for two months. Five dollars or one month."

Roddy made a sign to me as he left the dock, and I went down stairs to him.

"Get the money from Mollie and pay the fine for me, Barnes," he said, "don't let me be sent down. I have the money at home."

I went to Mollie and asked her to pay the fine; but she tossed her head at me and said; "It would serve him right, if I let him rot in jail, the brute."

I didn't have time to go back to Roddy then, as I had a good many things to look after, and I had promised my old woman to buy the goose—we had decided to have goose—for Christmas dinner, and I had to go on duty again at five o'clock, so Roddy slipped my memory, and I did not think of him again until next morning, when I thought I would go round to his house and wish him a happy Christmas. The house was all shut up and deserted, and one of the neighbors told me Roddy had not been home all night nor the day before either. I tried to rouse Mollie but could not make her hear. As I had nothing very particular to do for an hour or so, I thought I would go to the Central Station and see if Roddy's fine had been paid, or if he had been sent down.

Just as I expected, I found that Mollie had not been near Roddy, and that he had been sent down. Now, I suppose I am rather a foolish policeman, very likely I don't look at things in the way some people might think a right-minded policeman ought to view them, but I told you at the beginning of this story that I was not a machine and never would be, and it did seem to me pretty hard that poor Roddy should spend his Christmas in jail, so I just went home, got five dollars off the old woman—she is the cashier of our firm—went down to the jail and paid Roddy's fine.

"Thank you, kindly, old man," he said, "It was good of you to think of me and not let me spend Christmas in prison; Mollie might have paid the fine, there is more than fifty dollars in the house and she knows it. "I'll be round after dinner, old man, and give you the money."

I am partial to goose. I don't know whether it is

quite compatible with the dignity of a policeman to make such a confession, but I do like "the bird of folly," and am not ashamed to own it. I have a kind feeling for a goose too, and I think it a gross libel to call it the bird of folly; didn't a flock of geese save Rome, and Romulus and Remus, and Julius Cæsar, and Nero, and Reinzi, and all the other noble old Romans. Of course they did, or my Roman History tells a great big—no such thing. And if the geese hadn't saved Rome we couldn't have any Roman candles, or maccaroni, or Coliseum, or old Roman coins—made in Birmingham—now a days, could we? Of course not, so I don't think it fair to abuse the goose; I admire and respect the goose, especially when it is roasted with sage and onions and served up hot with nice rich gravy.

It was a model goose we had for our Christmas dinner, it weighed twelve pounds after it was cleaned and was as plump and fat as a partridge, and my old woman had done it to a turn. I like goose better than turkey, it is so much more filling and has more flavor in one drumstick than a turkey has in its whole body; besides there is a richness about it no turkey can ever have. I stood and looked fondly at that goose, and I felt a little sympathy for him—I suppose a policeman can feel sympathy for a goose without breaking the rules—as I thought how suddenly he had been cut off in the prime of his youth and goosehood; and I stood with the knife suspended over him for a moment, while the old woman and the children waited in longing expectation.

But I was not destined to carve that goose. Just as the knife was descending there came a sudden knock at the door, and before I could get to it it was opened, and Roddy burst into the room looking so wild and strange that I involuntarily dropped the knife and fork and exclaimed,

"For the Lord's sake, Roddy, what is the matter."

"They've gone," he gasped out. "Gone; come with me, Barnes, come with me and follow them."

"Who has gone?" I asked, "where do you want to go to?"

"Stop and take your dinner first, Roddy, whatever it might be," said my old woman, "I'm sure the goose is beautiful and you look most clammed."

"Mollie," said Roddy, not noticing my old woman's interruption, "Mollie has run away from me, and gone off with some fellow, taking everything they could lay their hands on. Come with me, old man, I must catch *him*."

I didn't like the way he emphasized that word "him," and the look on his face made me afraid to let him go alone. Still I did not like to leave the goose, and to gain time as much as anything else, I said :

"Tell us all about it, Roddy, what has happened?"

He stood silent for a moment as if to collect himself, and then said : "When you left me, Barnes, I

G

went home expecting to find Mollie; she was not at home, as usual, and I began to get things ready for dinner. In moving about the room I noticed that a good many things were gone, and everything seemed to have been tumbled about; I thought somebody had robbed the house while I was away—God knows I did not suspect Mollie then; I knew she was wild and careless, but I didn't think then she was as bad as I know now she is. Then I thought of the money; it was put between two bricks under the stove, and nobody knew where it was but Mollie and myself; the bricks were moved and the money gone. Barnes, old fellow, it came on me like a clap of thunder; she had run away from me!" Poor fellow, he stopped for a minute, and I could see big tears trying to come into his eyes, but sticking in his throat; he gulped them down and went on. "I asked some of the neighbours, and they told me she had gone away about an hour before in a sleigh with a swell-looking fellow in a fur coat and a big black moustache." Roddy was too much excited to be particular in his description, and did not stop to mention the other things the man must have been in. "One of the boys heard the man saying they would be in St. Johns in time for dinner, and then they drove away. Come with me, Barnes, I have a light cutter here and a good horse, we can catch them before they get to St. Albans."

I took another look at the goose. I liked Roddy, and I was willing to do anything I could for him, but I was hungry and the goose looked very tempting. Policemen like good things as well as other people, and I doubt that I should have given up the goose for Roddy's sake if it hadn't been for my old woman.

"Samuel," she said, "you had better go with Roddy." Roddy was a favourite with my old woman, altho' Mollie wasn't. "You may be wanted to arrest that thief and bring him back, for mark my words, he's no gentleman, but some loafer who has stolen some good clothes and run away with Mollie for what little money she could get. Take your dinner with you," she continued as she saw me look again at the goose, "and you and Roddy can eat it on the way," and before I could say a word she had seized the knife, cut both legs off the goose, folded them up in paper with several slices of bread, some butter, a screw of salt, a couple of knives, and stood with my coat all ready for me to put it on.

Of course I went; somehow I generally do what my old woman wants me to, and the last thing I heard as we drove away was my old woman calling out,

"Be sure you bring back the knives."

It was a long cold drive, and we talked very little on the way. We stopped for a minute at St. Lambert's, and took our dinner just as we left there, but the goose did not taste nearly as good as I expected, and as for Roddy he scarcely tasted a morsel, but

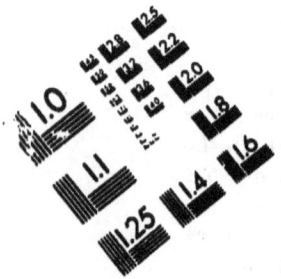
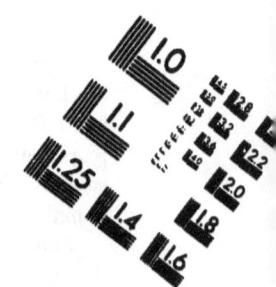

**IMAGE EVALUATION
TEST TARGET (MT-3)**

Photographic
Sciences
Corporation

23 WEST MAIN STREET
WEBSTER, N.Y. 14580
(716) 872-4503

kept lashing at the horse in a vicious kind of way, altho' there was really no occasion to touch him, for he was a good one to go and warmed up to his work first rate.

We heard of them at St. Johns. They had dined there and left about half an hour ahead of us. We made an effort to counterbalance that disadvantage by getting a fresh horse, as we found out they had not changed theirs.

Just as we were getting into the sleigh I made a discovery. Roddy's coat swung open for a moment as the wind caught it, and something hard struck my hand. I recognized the touch in an instant.

It was a pistol.

Then I remembered the queer way Roddy had said "I must catch him," and I gave myself a kind of a shake up as I said to myself: "Now look here, Mr. S. C. Barnes, Sub Constable, just attend to what you are about; if this here man shoots that there man it won't be pleasant for you; if you must go running after men who run away with other men's wives on Christmas Day, instead of staying at home and eating your hot goose like a sensible policeman, you must not let anybody get shot; for if you do some of those bothersome newspapers will get hold of it and give you a hauling over the coals about it, and you will find yourself in trouble. So look sharp and get hold of that pistol or look out for squalls."

It did not take me long to make up my mind what to do.

I asked Roddy to have a smoke and pulled out a
meerschaum, but in dragging out my coat tail to get
at my tobacco pouch I pulled Roddy's coat a little
away from his body, and quicker than I ever thought
I could have done it, I whipped the pistol out of his
pocket and put my pipe case in it. He drew his coat
up pretty quick and touched his side with his elbow,
but the pipe case felt all right, and he didn't suspect
anything.

If I had been asked two minutes before if I could
pick a pocket I should have laughed at the idea; but
after I had done it I could not help thinking either
that pocket picking was a good deal easier than is
generally supposed, or that a first-class pickpocket
was spoiled when I became a policeman.

We had not got more than about three miles out of
St. Johns when we sighted a sleigh just going round
a little bend in the road about a hundred yards ahead
of us, with three people in it; the driver and a man
and woman sitting pretty close together on the back
seat.

Roddy gave a start as he saw the sleigh, for he recognized Mollie; and I took that opportunity—the first
I had—to give the pistol a push off the seat on to the
bottom of the sleigh.

Now I never was partial to pistols; and I have
always specially objected to those self-cocking, self-
firing off things called revolvers. A good old-fashioned
horse-pistol that measures about half a yard or so in

length, takes a young steam engine to cock it, and a good strong kick by a full-grown bull to fire it off, I don't so much mind; that gives a man time and warning, so that there is a good square chance to dodge; but these revolving things always go off when they are not expected to, and nothing can persuade them to go off when wanted, if they don't happen to have a mind to.

Now, nobody wanted that pistol of Roddy's to go on when I touched, but off it went. Whether I pulled the trigger without knowing it, or whether it fell on the caps, or whether Roddy or I stepped on it and set it off there is no means of knowing now. All I do know is that two barrels of it *did* go off the minute I pushed it from the seat, and in another second our old horse had his tail up, the bit in his teeth and was tearing down that road at a pace that would have astonished Dexter; while Roddy gave a jump that nearly threw him out of the sleigh, and let a howl out of him loud enough to scare a whole churchyard. That miserable revolving machine had sent one ball through the dashboard, taking about four inches of skin and a handful of hair off the old horse's tail; and driven the other ball through the calf of Roddy's left leg. Then I made a grab at the reins, which Roddy had dropped, and moved my right foot in so doing, and the machine shot off again; but whether it did any damage or not I never found out, for by that time our horse had caught up with the sleigh ahead of us and tried to take the shortest cut out of reach of the shooting machine behind him by going over the sleigh, occupants and all.

The driver had heard our little bombardment and saw us coming; he tried all he could to give us room to pass and pulled well over into the snow bank on the left, but it was no use; the road was too narrow, and our horse, having nobody to guide him, did just what seemed best to his misguided fancy, and the last discharge of that miserable revolving machine had scarcely reverberated in his startled ears before we collided with the sleigh in front of us.

We struck about midships, as the sailors would say —at least I should judge so from the fact that our sleigh broke very nearly in half, and the old horse ran away with the front part while the back part was left with Roddy and I—but I could not be very certain of anything more than that we did strike; and that inside of half a second afterwards five feet nine and a half inches of policeman was describing a parabola through the air, and that just before he disappeared head first beneath the snow, he had a sort of vague and indistinct vision of a large flock of petticoats, buffalo robes, men's legs, splinters of sleighs, pieces of harness and other things, too numerous to mention, flying about in all directions; while the entire British Army, Volunteers and all, seemed to be firing a fusillade of joy at the event, such a tremendous noise did that miserable revolving machine make in letting off its last two shots.

How long it took me to get my head out of the snow, I can't tell; it felt like an hour, but I don't think it could have been over a minute, for the snow was soft, and although I went in far I came out easy. When I got up and looked around the first thing I saw was the tail of our old horse sticking up like a sign post, while he was tearing down the road like mad with the fragment of the sleigh behind him, and the other horse and sleigh, with two people in it, close after him. Then I looked to the left and saw a pair of legs trying to kick themselves out of the snow, so I got hold of one of them and gave it a good strong pull and brought out a smooth faced, red-headed man, I did not recognise, and as he sat down to recover himself I looked around for Roddy.

He had fallen under what portion of the sleigh was left us, and was partially stunned by a blow from some piece of the broken sleigh, and that added to the loss of blood from the wound in his leg had made him quite faint, so that it took some little time before I could bandage up his leg with my handkerchief and recover him a bit. He soon came to himself, and as quick as he recovered his senses he asked,

"Where is Mollie?"

I turned and pointed down the road when we could still see the race between our old horse and the other horse and sleigh, ours still having the best of it, and said,

"Gone."

He first looked at me for a second, and then with a
great cry he jumped past me, and the next thing I
saw was two men rolling over together in the snow,
tearing and fighting, and a black curly wig and big
black moustache lying in the road.

Of course I got at them at once and tried to separate them, but I should have had a poor chance if the
bandage hadn't slipped off Roddy's leg, and it began
to bleed again, so that he turned faint and loosed his
hold ; then I got out a pair of handcuffs I had in my
pocket and slipped them on the other man. Why I
did it, I couldn't have told, except that I was fighting
one to two, but I was glad of it afterwards. When he
found himself fast he just gave me a good hearty
curse or two, and then sat down on the broken sleigh
in a sullen manner and didn't say a word more.

It took me some time to quiet Roddy, and I don't
know how I could ever have got them both into St.
Johns if a farmer hadn't happened to drive up just
then, and I got him to help me and let me use his
sleigh.

We managed to hire a sleigh in St. Johns, and
after making arrangements for having the horse and
the remnants of the cutter sent after us, if our old
horse ever allowed himself to be caught, we started
for Montreal.

Before leaving, I searched my red-headed friend,
who proved, when he had his black wig and moustache
on, to be the same man who had spoken to me on

William Street the morning before, and found
Roddy's watch and fifty-five dollars in money on him,
part of which Roddy identified, so I was all safe in
taking him back.

It was near midnight when we got to Montreal,
and I had my man lodged in the Chaboillez Square
Police Station, and then I took Roddy home with
me, and my old woman fixed us up a bit of hot supper, and I took a drop of something warm, for I had
to go to the Ottawa Station and report for duty as
soon as possible; but Roddy wouldn't touch a drop of
anything although he must have been pretty cold.

"I've had my last drink, old man," he said, "to-
day's business has sobered me for life. Perhaps Mollie would have proved a better wife to me by and by
if I had kept straight, and not taken to drink again.
Poor girl, I must go to St. Albans after her to-morrow, Barnes. I can't let her go to the bad this way
without making one effort to save her. She can't be
all bad yet, and I haven't behaved any too well to
her lately. I must see her again."

Poor fellow, he pushed away the plate of hot gib-
blets and other remnants of the goose which my old
woman had put before him, without having more
than tasted it, and sat with his head on his hands
quite sorrowful. Somehow the goose seemed to stick
in my throat, and I felt very much like I was going
to cry, which would have been very undignified in a
policeman, when my old woman cut in with,

"Samuel, you did not bring back the knives. I knew you wouldn't."

It was a fact, and worse than that I had lost my pipe, an old pet meerschaum which had been a good friend to me for years; the case was all safe in Roddy's pocket, but my good old pipe was gone. So was Roddy's shooting machine, but I did not care about that, and felt rather glad than otherwise that it was at a safe distance where it couldn't go off without warning and shoot somebody.

Next morning I was at the Central Station early to make my deposition, and there I made an agreeable discovery. I discovered that I had made a great capture; that my red headed friend was no less a personage than Mr. William Sinclair, alias Dick Smith, alias Augustus Hamilton, against whom three or four warrants had been issued in Toronto and Hamilton, and for whose arrest a reward of $1,000 was offered. It appeared that Sinclair had been clerk in a large business house in Hamilton, and had robbed his employers of several thousand dollars, but had managed it so cleverly that it was some time after he left before it was discovered. Meanwhile he had gone to Toronto, where he passed under the name of Dick Smith, and there forged two cheques for about fifteen hundred dollars on the National Sand Bank of that city; having accomplished which he had run off with the wife of one of the Bank clerks, and had been tracked to the States, where all trace

of him was lost, and he was supposed to have gone to
California. This was about a year before I saw him;
our detectives here had been on the look out for him
at the time, and had his description, photograph, &c.,
but the scent had grown pretty cold, and when Mr.
Augustus Hamilton appeared in Montreal as a gentleman "just out from the old country," he was not
suspected. What he wanted in Montreal, or whether
he had committed any robbery here never transpired, as no charge was made against him, Roddy re-
fusing to prosecute when he found there were already
so many more serious crimes for him to answer for.
He was transferred to Toronto, where he was tried
and condemned to grace the Penitentiary for seven
years, and he is still there, his close cropped red
head being much admired, and being quite an ornament to the place.

Roddy went to St. Albans as soon as his leg was
better, but could not find Mollie, who had gone on to
New York. He followed her there, and found her so
much worse than he expected that he left her to follow her evil courses and went to California, where he
remained for a couple of years.

Two Christmasses came and went, and I made my
dinner off that noble bird the goose in peace and comfort, without interruption; and the third one was
well on its way to us when one fine night, just as my
old woman and I and a large number of small Bar-
neses were sitting down to supper, in walked Roddy

looking so bronzed and stout that for a moment I hardly knew him.

He told us all his adventures, which were very interesting to us, but would most likely only bore you as they were principally an account of hard work, so I shall not repeat them. Enough to say that he had tried gold mining a while, found it didn't pay, and had finally settled down to his old trade in San Francisco, where he could make from four to six dollars a day. But he did not like the place, and had just returned to Montreal, bringing a couple of thousand dollars with him, with the intention of setting up in business for himself.

All the time he was talking I could see that my old woman was itching to ask him a question, I knew what, for there was one name he had never mentioned, and at last she could keep back no longer but blurted it right out:

"Roddy, what has become of Mollie?"

He grew very pale for an instant, but said quite softly and reverently, "Dead. She died six months ago in a brothel in St. Louis. Poor girl, may God be merciful to her for her sin, and forgive me my share in making her what she turned out to be, a drunkard and a prostitute. Yes, old man, a good deal of it was my fault. I ought to have been kinder to her, and checked her flirting ways gently, instead of getting into mad fits of jealousy as I used to. Oh, you never knew half of the quarrels we had, although, thank God, I never struck her but once. Yes, old man, I was some to blame, I was not steady enough to marry such a young girl; she was pretty and fond of admiration, and it was only natural when I made a beast of myself by getting drunk and abusing her, that she should turn to some one else. Poor girl, let us leave her memory in peace, I can't bear to talk much about her."

We didn't say another word, but my old woman got up and went to the cupboard, and very soon came back with something in a glass which smoked and smelled very refreshing, which she put by his side and said,

"Take a drop of something hot, Roddy, it will warm your stomach and cheer you up a bit."

Somehow my old woman has a notion that there is no remedy in the world for any complaint, whether mental or physical, like " a drop of something warm ;" and I think if I was taken home some night with my neck broken or my brains knocked out, my old woman would administer, " a drop of something warm to cheer me up a bit;" but Roddy pushed the glass from him and said gently, but firmly,

"Thank you kindly, Mrs. Barnes, but since the last night I was in your house, I have not tasted a drop of strong liquor, and with God's help, I never will again. I don't say anything against a man taking a glass if he can control himself, but I can't; if I drink at all I must drink too much, and then I am more like a devil than a man, so the only safe plan for me is to swear off altogether and I have done it. Drink and jealousy together nearly made me commit one murder—you know, old man—and I can't but feel that is partly responsible for Mollie's death. No, I have taken the pledge, and I mean to keep it."

And he has to this day.

You need not ask for Sub-Constable Barnes in the force after New Years, for I have sent in my resignation; but if you want any plumbing or glazing done just look for the firm of Duckworth & Barnes in the directory and give us a call; and we'll plumb you and glaze you as reasonable as any people in the business. And if you are anywhere in my neighborhood on Christmas Day stay where you are and don't come bothering me for I want to eat my goose in peace, and I don't know but what you may want to run away with my old woman, and then I should have another chase after a runaway couple on Christmas Day. So stay at home like a good fellow, eat your own goose and I'll wish you a good appetite to enjoy it with, and a Merry Christmas and a Happy New Year after.

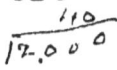

Out of the Gutter.

H

OUT OF THE GUTTER.

CHAPTER I.

RUN OVER.

It certainly was not a pleasant Christmas. Even the most joyful observer of that cheerful time could not derive any comfort or encouragement from the dull, leaden, overcast sky; the dripping clouds and the slight flurries of snow which melted to slush as it touched the filthy streets, ankle deep in mud and filth and running streams of dirty water. The trees sighed mournfully and tossed their branches about in the moaning wind with a dismal, despairing action; the sun hid his face as if ashamed of himself that the weather should be unpropitious for Christmas. The bells were ringing out for church, and straggling streams of rain-drenched, limp and draggled figures, fighting manfully with unruly umbrellas, were threading St. Catherine, Dorchester and numerous cross streets on their way to the different churches. Now

and again a sleigh would drive by; but, it didn't have
the merry, cheery ring which a sleigh ought to have;
the horses' hoofs splashed heavily into the sodden
street, and the runners cut gratingly through the
half frozen snow and muck. No cheerful voices rang
out, no gay laugh or light jest broke upon the ear; the
driver sat crouched in a heap on his seat with cap
drawn over his eyes, and head bent to the drifting
sleet; the occupants huddled together as if for warmth,
and presented a mingled mass of draggled furs, soaked
garments and demoralized umbrellas.

No well-disposed, self-respecting umbrella could
sustain itself in an upright, independent way, as if it
rather liked to be rained on, on such a day; the
downpour of rain, snow, sleet and hail, coming in
quick succession, so quick as to appear to come all
together, was enough to discourage any umbrella, and
none of them made an effort to hold up their heads in
a defiant manner, as umbrellas sometimes will on a
hot day or during a short summer shower. Some
sagged limply down between the ribs and poured
little streams, like miniature waterfalls, on unprotected
passers by or neighboring umbrellas; some displayed
broken ribs sticking out in an apologetical sort of way
as if to say "I would be very smart and independent
of wind and weather, but you see my careless master
has broken my pet rib, and what can you expect of an
umbrella with a broken rib;" some lacked a ferrule;
the seams of others grinned open in a dispairing fashion

as if they had held on to the silk, or cotton, as long as umbrella nature could stand it, and now were forced to give up from exhaustion; some had great rents in them, and served merely as conduits for plentiful streams of water to pour on the misguided carriers who fondly believed they were being protected; all had a disheartened, discouraged appearance, and seemed to express, as well as umbrellas can express, their opinion that it was not at all what Christmas ought to be.

In all that crowd there was only one umbrella that seemed to have any self-assertion; only one which held its own firmly and bravely against the weather, not in a bragging, boastful manner, but in a resolute, determined way as if it knew it was simply doing its duty and did not intend to allow any sort of wind or weather to prevent it. A dogged-looking sort of an umbrella, not particularly pleasant to look at but withal presenting a very useful appearance; an umbrella that had seen service, as its faded color, and a very perceptible patch, and the well-worn ferrule testified, but one that was still ready to do duty for years, if treated to a new cover, as the strong whalebone ribs, heavy blackthorn stick, and massive buckhorn handle showed. A resolute, serviceable umbrella made for use not show, and in admirable keeping with the man who carried it.

He was a tall, well-built, compact man of forty-five or fifty years of age, with clustering black hair, just tinged with grey, brushed back from his high wide forehead; and trim side-whiskers displaying to advantage a square deep chin and a mouth rather above the average size with firm, but kindly lines about it. His eyes were of that nondescript kind of grey commonly known as "cat's eyes," and their expression was partly hidden by a pair of spectacles. His dress betokened him a clergyman, and his rapid pace showed that he was a little late for service. He hurried along St. Catherine Street and had almost reached the cross street where his church was situated when, suddenly, a loud shout fell on his ears;

"Hi, look out there!"

In another instant a sharp scream of agony pierced the air; there was a vision of a sleigh rapidly disappearing down a cross street, the driver standing up and lashing his horse almost to madness in his anxiety to escape, and of a crushed, moaning, cursing mass of humanity lying in a heap on the street, round which a small crowd had already begun to assemble.

Pushing his way through the wet figures and discouraged umbrellas the clergyman advanced to the figure and bent beside it.

What was it? Was it a small man or a large boy; was it human, or was it some terrible monstrosity bearing the semblance of man?

The figure was doubled up in agony, and the helpless, awkward manner in which the right leg lay showed that it was broken; a ragged cap had fallen off and revealed an unkempt head of long black hair, matted and dirty and soiled with the mud of the street; half peering out from shaggy eyebrows and the masses of dark hair shone a pair of piercing black eyes, almost glaring with mingled rage and pain as it shook its doubled fist at the retreating sleigh. It was the figure of a boy, with the face of a demon and the garb of a man.

A pair of worn-out top-boots, with holes in the soles and the toes peeping out of the uppers, encased his legs and received into them the bottoms of a pair of pants many sizes too large for the wearer; a rough pilot jacket, out at elbows and in the last stages of decay, generally completed his outer garments, and he seemed to have nothing under but a ragged and dirty cotton shirt, soiled portions of which could be seen through the rents in his coat and pants. He was writhing terribly in his agony, and mingling with his groans, fierce oaths and horrible execrations against the driver of the sleigh which had run over him.

"Cuss you, cuss you," he shouted as he tried to raise himself and fell back exhausted—"Oh, God, my back's broke! Oh! oh! he's killed me, cuss him, if I aint dead I'm crippled for life; won't nobody catch the murderin' thief an' hang him; where's the perlese? they's alwers round after poor boys like me when they ain't wanted, —— them, where's they now?"

"Where are you hurt, my poor boy?" inquired the clergyman kindly. "Are any bones broken?"

"I'm broken all over," groaned the boy; "Cuss him, he done it a purpose, I see him drive right at me as I was a crossing the street; he's broke me leg an' me back, an' I 'most think me neck's broke."

"Not quite so bad as that, let us hope," rejoined the clergyman mildly, "come, try to get up, let me help you." He placed one arm gently under the boy's shoulders and tried to lift him, but the pain proved too great for the little sufferer and he fell back fainting.

The crowd, which had by this time grown to a considerable size, now began to find their tongues and offered aimless bits of advice, and threw out suggestions of impossible things which ought to be done, in that reckless manner which usually characterizes a crowd hastily drawn together by an accident. Several suggestions to "send for the police" were made but nobody went, everybody seeming to think it was somebody else's business to go; propositions were made to "run after the wretch and stop him" (meaning the carter) but none stirred; one excited little barber, who had darted out of a neighboring shop with a shaving-brush filled with lather in his hand, offered to "give the alarm," but as it was not made clear that the firemen were needed, the suggestion was not acted on; and one lady, whose appearance gave evidence that she ought to have remained at home, declared that it had given her a "turn" from which she did not expect to recover until a certain interesting event had transpired, and then she would not be surprised if " it " was marked with a sleigh and a horse trampling down a boy; which announcement called forth a sigh of commiseration from some of the female bystanders.

The only persons in the crowd who seemed to have their wits about them were the clergyman, who was kneeling in the mud to the utter destruction of his new black pants, supporting the boy's head; and a bare-footed, bonnetless, ragged little crossings-sweeper who had made her way to the front and stood leaning on her broom looking at the injured boy.

" It's jest like them drivers," she said, " they alwers runs over boys an' girls. Why don't they run down fokes as is their own size an' cud take their own part. Shall I run fur a sleigh, sir ?" she continued, turning to the clergyman, "there's a stan' near by."

"Yes, if you please, my good girl; make haste, he ought to be taken to the hospital at once."

" All right, boss" cried the girl, and darted round the corner at a run.

"I ain't goin' to no hosspittle," said the boy, in a voice weak from pain, just recovering from his swoon. " I don't want nobody a cuttin' me up, an' I don't want no skilley. I ain't a pauper, an' I wants to be took home to my own house."

" Where is that ?" inquired the clergyman.

" Briggs's Yard, off Kempt Street."

" What is your name ?"

"Billy the toad."

"What?"

"That's what the boys calls me. Me right name's Billy Taylor. Oh, me back's broke —— ——" and then followed a terrible volley of oaths making the blood run cold in the veins of at least one listener as he heard the horrible imprecations falling from the lips of one so young.

"Hush, hush, my boy; you must not use such fearful words."

"Why mustn't I cuss him; what did he want to run over me fur?"

Further conversation was prevented by the arrrival of a sleigh with the little crossings-sweeper hanging on behind, who immediately announced her return by exclaiming

"Here we are, boss."

The injured boy was with difficulty lifted into the sleigh and covered with buffalo robes, not, however, without his indulging in another volley of oaths until pain again overcame him and he became insensible for the second time.

"Take him to his home, Briggs's Yard, off Kempt Street," said the clergyman to the carter, "it will be better, perhaps, for him to be with his parents; and then take this card to Dr. Homecraft, Beaver Hall Hill, and ask him to attend to the boy at once, it would be best for you to take the doctor to the house, then return to me and I will pay you; here is my address." The carter looked at the card handed him and read "Rev. Charles Chessworth, D. D., LL.D., No. — St. Catherine Street."

"All right, your honor, I'll see him all safe," said cabby, getting into his seat.

"Can't I go with him, yer rivirince?" asked the little crossings-sweeper. "I knows his fokes." This assertion was a base fabrication, but Mr. Chessworth did not know that and smiled consent while he said,

"Take good care of him my little woman, and tell his parents I will call to-morrow or next day."

"You bet, boss," was the rejoinder, as she clambered into the sleigh, broom and all. "Oh, crickey, ain't this style, oh, no, not at all?"

CHAPTER II.

BRIGGS'S YARD.

The Reverend Charles Chessworth, for the first time in his life, kept his congregation waiting that morning and entered hot and flustered with his rapid walk and quick change of garments; but his parishioners all agreed that never before had he preached so eloquently, never before had he gone home so closely to their hearts and waked in them so deep a sense of the thanks they owed to the Almighty for his infinite mercy and goodness; and when he referred to the accident which had detained him, and described in terse but earnest terms the scene he had witnessed and how the boy had been almost cut off in his sins with words of profanation on his lips, many an eye grew moist, and many a silent prayer for strength to repent while there was yet time was breathed, and many a mental vow was taken, let us hope, to be firmly kept.

The service was over, and the rector sat in the vestry slowly putting on his gloves preparatory to leaving when the carter he had sent with the boy entered and gave him a note; it ran as follows:

"DEAR CHARLES,

Come and see the boy you sent for me to attend, as soon as possible. I am afraid I can be of little service to him, and he is sadly in need of you. It is a queer case.

Yours,
GEORGE HOMECRAFT."

The rector pulled out his watch and looked at it; it was half-past one, and a little sigh escaped him as he thought of his tempting Christmas dinner which would be ready in an hour, and which he would now, probably have to postpone. Don't smile at him; rectors are but human, and a light breakfast had tended to make the Rev. Charles hungry, but he stifled the selfish wish, and finishing pulling on his gloves grasped the reliable umbrella in his hand, followed the carter out, and desired him to drive again to Briggs's Yard.

It is an old time-worn saying that "one half of the world does not know how the other half lives," but I am pretty confident that one half of the inhabitants of Montreal do not even dream how the other half live, nor where they live. It would be a good lesson to some of us to visit a few of the "yards" off the bye-streets and lanes of this city, hidden away from the general public and scarcely noticed by the transient passer-by, where the poorest of the poor live; to witness the poverty, privation, want and filth in which thousands of the lower classes drag out their existence—living it can scarcely be called—would tend to make many an one content with his lot, who now grumbles at his position, and thinks himself thoroughly wretched because he cannot command some of the higher and daintier luxuries of life. To witness the abject destitution, the utter absence of even what are usually considered the necessities of life, the squalid filth and total want of comfort in which these people exist, would cause a feeling of astonishment that they can manage to subsist at all, and of thankfulness for our own place in the world. It is but a short time since the community was shocked by the recital in the newspapers of the terrible tragedy in Tabb's yard; and astonishment was expressed in the press that people could live in such a wretched place. I have visited the spot and I say that bad as it is it is clean and comfortable as compared with some of the yards in Griffintown and in other portions of the city.

Briggs's Yard was far from being an exception to the general rule of these yards, except that it might possibly be a little more delapidated, a little more squalid and the inhabitants a little dirtier than most of the others. The entrance to it was from Kempt Street, and the yard itself was about a hundred feet long by thirty deep; on to this space, which served as a general repository for all the waste and garbage of the tenants, opened, on two sides, the fronts of the houses comprising the yard proper, while the third side was occupied by the wood sheds &c. of the yard, and the fourth side by the sinks and out-houses of the houses fronting on Kempt Street, whose noisome odors furnished the only perfume to be found in that locality. The yard itself was now ankle deep in mud and slush and half-melted snow which lay deep on the ground; and as the merciful covering which concealed the putrifying filth below slowly melted away, heaps of decaying animal and vegetable matter, offal, scraps, bones, rotten potatoes, and cabbage leaves, cats, and a dog far gone in the stages of decomposition, obtruded themselves on the eye and became obnoxiously palpable to the nose.

The houses were old, delapidated, tumble-down shanties of two stories high, built of wood with shingle roofs which had been patched and mended in some places, and sagged down uncomfortably in others in a manner highly suggestive of a sudden collapse; they were innocent of paint but were black with age, and smoke, and mould, and mildew, and many of them were in so weak and worn-out a condition that they had had to be propped up in various places to induce them to retain something like an upright position; but no power short of pulling them down and building them over again could induce them to stand upright, and they all hung a little forward in a tired, worn-out way as if they had grown weary of remaining so long in so wretched a place and longed to lie at length on the ground and be cut up as firewood and carried off to be burnt in stoves and so end their miserable

existences. Around all these houses ran ricketty, old
balconies which were reached by crazy, worm-eaten,
slippery, foot-worn stairs, which creaked and groaned
under the lightest footstep as if protesting against
further ill-usage; and these stairs led to the upper
parts of the houses, which were occupied by different
families from the lower parts—the entrances to
which were on the level of the yard—few residents
of the yard being rich or exclusive enough to occupy
an entire house.

About twenty families pigged it together in B   gs's
yard, and the whole population turned out to witness
the arrival of so distinguished a personage as "the
pa'son" who had been sent for to visit "Billy the
toad."

Crowding on the ricketty balconies, at the imminent risk of breaking them down, were dozens of
shaggy-bearded, coatless, rough-looking men, and
unkempt slatternly women, many of them with babes
in their arms; while peering out from behind the
dresses of the women, peeping between the frowsy
pants of the men, and gazing through the bars of the
balcony appeared the eager faces of scores of shock-
headed children, watching and listening with all their
eyes and ears to catch every word and see every
action of the visitor. Very quiet and respectful were
the inhabitants of the yard, but very observant also;
and remarks, not altogether complimentary, were
passed on the visitor's legs—which one lady affirmed,

soto voce, "were bow-legged to that degree you could shove a wheelbarrow between 'em an' not touch his trouses;" on his spectacles, on his coat, on his heavy boots, and even on his umbrella, which one young female—whose hair was rather dishevelled, and whose shoes were considerably down at the heel—pronounced a "pokey" affair. These remarks were not intended for the visitor's ears; but, nevertheless, some of them reached him as he inquired the way to "Mr. Taylor's," and was shown up a creaking stair which he was told led to the chamber where "Billy the toad" was.

It was the shabbiest and meanest of all the shabby and mean houses in the yard, into which the Rev. Charles Chessworth was ushered, and he had scarcely reached the balcony when a dirty little face was pushed out of the doorway and a sharp voice accosted him with,

"Come along, your rivirince, I'll show 'um to yer. He's took awful bad."

"Ah, there you are, my little woman, shew me where the boy is."

At the rear of the room into which the balcony opened was a short ladder leading to a little cubby hole, or half attic in the roof, and there, lying on a dirty bed, was the boy who had been run over in the morning.

The Rev. Charles Chessworth was accustomed to visit the dwellings of the poor; he was not one of your kid-gloved clergymen who pay delicate and polite attention to the souls of the rich and endeavor to save them in a gentlemanly way, but leave the poor to take care of themselves; he believed in carrying hope and consolation to those who needed it most without any respect to persons, he was, therefore, prepared to find misery and poverty, but it appeared to him as he entered the room that he had never been in so wretched a hole before.

The room was small, scarce eight feet square, and the sloping roof came down to the floor making it difficult to stand erect anywhere except close to the door; the floor was rotten and creaked unpleasantly when trod on, while great gaps and seams in the shingle roof afforded glimpses of the heavy sky, and gave an opportunity for the rain to stream down in continuous little rivulets. The sides of the room were dank and mildewed, and the smell of decaying wood filled the place. Furniture there was scarce any; a broken down bedstead minus a leg, the place of which was supplied by an old box; a ricketty chair without a bottom; a few old boxes, a barrel, some blacking jugs and a basket being all there was in the room, except two bundles of rags in corners which looked as if they may be used for beds, and gave the impression that three persons occupied this small room. Fire there was none, nor any place for making one, and the scantiness of the filthy covering on the bed caused one to wonder that any human being could sleep there during our long, cold winter nights and not freeze to death.

The boy was lying on the bed with his eyes closed as the clergyman entered, but he opened them on hearing a step, and tried to turn himself a little so as to face his visitor, but the effort cost him a groan. There was no one in the room save the little girl who showed the way and Mr. Chessworth dispatched her on an errand, and drawing the bottomless chair to the bedside placed the head of the barrel across it and seated himself by the boy.

"How do you feel now, my boy?"

"Awful bad, sir; I'm broke all to pieces. Did they catch the murderin' thief, cuss him?" and then followed another string of oaths against the carter.

"My boy, do you know that you are in great danger; that your life is despaired of, and that in a few hours you may be in the presence of your Maker; are you not afraid to die with such sinful thoughts on your mind, such dreadful words on your lips?"

"I aint afraid of nothin'. What's the good of bein' a frighten' Friday."

"Don't you fear God's anger?"

"Whose he? He never done nothin' fur me; what should I care fur him fur?"

"Do you know what day this is?"

"Yes, it's Christmas, an' there aint no papers to sell, worse luck."

"Do you know why we commemorate Christmas Day?"

"I dunno; some of the boys said the first bull was killed Christmas Day, an' that's why people alwers eats roast beef an' plum puddin' that day, only I never gets none."

"Did you never hear of the Saviour who was born on this day to save sinners; were you never at Church?"

"No. Church ain't for the likes o' me; if I hang about the door for a little while an' thinks of goin' in, the perlese alwers drives me off; church is fur rich folks as can wear clean closes and pay the pa'son, poor boys aint got no business there."

"Did your parents never send you to school?"

"I never had no parents; I was born by chance, an' me aunt bringed me up 'till I cud work fur misself, an' then I selled papers an' blacked boots opposite the Hall, only the perlese was alwers a drivin' me off; they's drefful hard on a poor boy."

"And you never had any education?"

"Dunno what that is."

"Did you never learn to read or write?"

"I learn'd to read, me an' Spotty can spell out some of the big letters in the papers; Spotty went to school at nights, he did, but they licked him too much an' he don't go no more now."

"Who is Spotty?"

"He's me brother; his name's Jim, but the boys calls him Spotty. He's two years younger nor me, but he's partners with me now, he does the rounds an' I sells on the street."

"How do you live?"

"Me an' Spotty an' Snails keeps house here," the boy's voice had a touch of pride in it as he said this, "we pays Mrs. Mullins a dollar a month fur this room, an' we grubs ourselfs. We aint loafers, we aint, we pays our way. Say — " he added suddenly, "how long is I goin' to be laid up here? I aint got much money an' I must work perty soon, I aint goin' to loaf on Spotty an' Snails. I don't feel no pain now, I can't be very bad."

"You will be ill for some time, I am afraid; perhaps you may never recover."

"Well, I can't help that, it aint much use a poor boy living no how."

"You are very young, my boy, to have such opinions; how old are you?"

"I dunno; I 'spose I'm about a dozen."

Just then Dr. Homecraft, who had been for some splints, returned and set the broken leg. He represented the boy's case as dangerous, as he feared some internal injury, but said that with care he might recover, although it would be a long time before he would be able to work again.

Both men tried hard to induce the boy to allow himself to be taken to the hospital; he opposed the idea for a long time, but at last, having extracted a promise that he should not be " cut up " and have no " skilley " he consented, and arrangements were made for removing him at once.

The Rev. Charles gave up all idea of a pleasant Christmas dinner and sat down by the boy to read to him while Dr. Homecraft made the preparations for taking him to the hospital. Very gently, very lovingly, the rector read and talked to that boy, endeavouring to instil into his mind the truths of the Gospel. Very kindly and very lovingly he tried to let in some light on that dark soul and expose to it some of the beauties of Christianity. Very tenderly and very feelingly he drew the picture of the birth of the Lamb of God on this day eighteen centuries ago, and unfolded the plan by which sinful man was to be reinstated in favor with his Creator. Very simply and very touchingly he spoke, and a prayer went up from his own heart as the blessed words fell from his lips, that the light of truth may be shed on this dark mind, and that Christ might not have died in vain for this poor soul.

He used no flowers of speech, he tried none of the arts of oratory; he spoke plainly, feelingly, touchingly, and the boy listened; listlessly, unheedingly at first, but gradually becoming more interested as if he was hearing some pleasant tale, and something like a smile of hope, a flush of expectancy stole over his face as he asked:

"Do you think I'd have any chance? I ain't a very bad 'un; I never stole nothin', an' I don't lie much nor swear 'cept when I'm mad, an' I never was took up fur loafin' but on'st. Do yer think there's any chance fur me?"

"No one can be so wicked; no one can be so lost or depraved but what there is a chance for him in God's mercy, if he will only try to avail himself of it."

"I'd like to be respect'ble," said the boy, half musingly, "I'd like to wear good clothes, an' wash clean, an' be like some other boys I sees; not them as blacks boots an' sells papers, but them as goes to school an' goes to church, an' gets rich when they grows up. Do you think I'se got a chance?"

"There is a chance of success in this world for all who are honest and sober, and who are willing to work hard to deserve success. Will you try?"

"Yes, I'll try. I ain't afraid of work, an' I ken keep sober if I likes."

"Then we'll make a bargain. You go to the hospital and try to get well, I will come to see you, and when you are strong again I will see if I cannot help you to 'a chance' for a better life in the future. If God in his mercy spares your life I will try to afford you the 'chance' you ask to make that life good and useful; will you try to make good use of that 'chance'?"

"I'll do the best I can, boss; I'll try as hard as I know how."

CHAPTER III.

MANY YEARS AFTER.

It was a long and desperate fight between life and death before " Billy the toad," was pronounced out of danger; and the long winter had passed away and the first breath of spring was perfuming the earth ere he was strong enough to leave the hospital, and even then he was very pale and weak and not able to do any work.

A great change had come over the boy; during his illness Dr. Chessworth had been unremitting in his kindness and attention, paid him frequent visits, loaned him books to read which he was capable of understanding, and gradually laid the foundation for training the mind at the same time that the body was slowly recovering. When Billy left the hospital his good friend, the rector, got him a place on a farm in the Eastern Townships, and the country air and exercise soon restored him to health; but he never went back on the streets to earn a living; the good seed which had be enplanted that Christmas Day that seemed the darkest in his life bore good fruit, and Briggs's yard knew him no more.

Years of quiet, patient, earnest plodding, and of hard honest labor in a country village gave him, by the time he reached manhood, a good position in the business he was engaged in, and his employer talked of giving him a share in the business; but he had set his heart on other things, and at the age of twenty-two, having saved money enough to pay his expenses, he resigned his position, and entered college to study for the church.

He was a quick and ready scholar and progressed rapidly, for the acquirement of learning had been the one pleasure of his life, and he had for years devoted all his spare time to study, so that when he entered college he knew more than most men do when they leave. The same energy and spirit of independence which has characterised him as a boy clung to him as a man, and he soon became noticed as one who would make his mark in the world. How true that prophecy will prove remains yet to be seen; but he bids fair to fulfill it.

Last Christmas morning there was a larger attendance than usual at Dr. Chessworth's church to hear the preaching of a young missionary who had just returned from the Hudson Bay Territory, where he had been two years; and it was well understood that he would probably be offered the position of assistant to Dr. Chessworth, whose age and declining health rendered him scarcely able to do the work of the parish alone. From the moment he began to preach the attention of the congregation was seized and never flagged to the end; but long ere that point was reached it was settled in the minds of his hearers that he was a man worthy to assist, and possibly, in the course of time, to succeed the good pastor who had for so many years presided over them.

It was a very pleasant party which assembled at the good rector's house that night, and not the least brilliant amongst the throng was the Reverend William Taylor, the "Billy the toad" of former years, and hanging on his arm was a beautiful and modest young woman whose slight blush at being addressed as "Mrs. Taylor," showed that matrimony was still new to her, and in whom I afterwards discovered— when this story was told me by the rector—the little crossings-sweeper of years gone by.

"And where is your brother Jim?" I asked of the Rev. Taylor, who was present.

"There, I hope and believe," he answered, reverently pointing upwards, "Jim has been called away early," he continued, "but we have the consolation of knowing that there is every reasonable belief that he was called to a better life than this. Ah, doctor," he went on, turning to Dr. Chessworth and speaking with great feeling, "What do I not owe you; what might I not have been but for your kindness and goodness to me when you took me out of the gutter."

Jones, the Lawyer.

JONES, THE LAWYER.

CHAPTER I.

MR. JONES.

Plain " Jones, the lawyer," had his office in one of the buildings situate on St. James street, between St. Gabriel street and Place d'Armes hill on the right hand side of the street, going east.

I call him "Plain" Jones, not because he is plain; nor because that is his proper and peculiar Christian cognomen; nor because it is a nickname he has acquired; nor because he is so recorded in the directory; nor because he is ever so addressed. I call him Plain Jones because he is always alluded to as "Jones, the lawyer," without any special reference to any particular Christian name; and as any definite appropriation of a Christian name to him is at present unnecessary, I will call him, for a while "Plain" Jones.

Plain Jones had an office in one of those queer looking houses on what used to be called "Little" St. James street, which now present so curious an appearance since the sidewalk on that side of the street

has been lowered, and look as if they were ashamed
of themselves for allowing a part of their foundations
to be exposed, and were quite shocked at the idea of
three or four little wooden steps being tacked on to
them to enable people to reach their entrance doors;
somewhat resembling the little flight of moveable
steps which formed the means of access to the lofty
four-post bedsteads of our boyhoods' days.

Plain Jones was a lawyer; but you must not suppose he had any such plebian word exposed on the
outer part of his office door: no, there he was described
as an "Advocate."

It is a curiously noticeable fact that although there
are about one hundred or more persons who have
offices on the two blocks between St. Gabriel street
and Place d'Armes hill, who get their living by "the
study and practice of the law," there is not a single
sign showing that there is a lawyer on the street.
You will find "Advocates," "Notaries," "Commis-
sioners," without number, but not a sign with the
word "Lawyer" on it. Now why is this? I have
looked up the two words, lawyer and advocate, in
Webster's dictionary with the following result:

LAWYER, *n.* [that is *lawer*, contracted from *law-wer*,
law-man.] One versed in the laws, or a practitioner
of law; one whose profession is to institute suits in
courts of law, and to prosecute or defend the cause of
clients.

ADVOCATE, *n* [L. *advocatus.*] One who pleads the

cause of another before any tribunal or judicial court.

Now the only practical difference I can see between the two definitions is that a lawyer is "one *versed* in the laws, and an advocate is "one who pleads the cause for another before any tribunal or judicial court." perhaps that may be the reason why there are so many advocates and so few lawyers. And that is the reason I have called my hero, "Jones, the lawyer," for although he had "advocate" over his door he was a "lawyer," and a good one too, for he was "one versed in the laws."

Plain Jones had his office on the second floor, just at the head of the stairs, at the back, and the door, from which the paint had long ago peeled off, butted out at you in an offensive sort of way as you reached the top step. It was an antagonistic sort of door which seemed on the face of it to say, "You'll find it a pretty hard matter to get the better of me." And so it proved, if you tried to open it; for it was a difficult door to open and deceived you on the start, the knob turning round and round in your hand without causing any perceptible effect on the latch. After you had pulled two or three times you discovered that the latch was an entirely independent affair from the knob, and was controlled by a little iron flange, just big enough to accommodate your thumb, which protruded in a cautious sort of way, only a few inches from the door, a little below the knob. When you got your thumb on the little iron flange and tried to raise the latch, you would find that your difficulties were not over; for the flange was worn very smooth and your thumb would slide off, unless you were very careful; and when you had a good purchase on it you would have to pull the door a little to you by the knob with the other hand, for the latch was stiff and would not come up without a struggle; and then some-one would probably call out from inside "pull hard." After a tug or two the door would open in a sullen way, as much as to say, "Very well, my friend, you *would* get in, mind, it is not my fault if you find it harder to get out."

Some people did say it was harder to get out of Plain Jones' hands than to get into them, for he bore the reputation of being rather harder to deal with even than his door was; as a good many people had found out during the twenty odd years he had practised at the bar.

But Plain Jones was not a dry, musty old lawyer at all. He was plump and round faced and oily looking, with a fine high forehead, slightly bald about the temples, a wipe head of kinky hair, almost white, which he wore well brushed back, a merry, twinkling blue eye, and a jolly, good-natured expression. He had full whiskers shaved all round, leaving the mouth and chin quite clean, which disclosed the fact that he had a slight double chin, with a merry little dimple on it which winked rougishly at you. His whiskers had once been red—auburn, I suppose I ought to say—but were now so sprinkled with white that they looked a light straw color, and gave the appearance of a fringe around his face. Taken altogether he was as pleasant-looking a middle-aged gentleman, a little on the right side of fifty, as could be found in a day's search; and generally wore a quiet, cheerful little smile which was very refreshing to see. He was scrupulously neat and particular about his dress, and always had a clean, polished-up look, like a thorough-bred horse after being properly groomed.

Plain Jones was a bachelor—of his own free will, he would take pains to inform you, and not through any obduracy of the fair sex—and openly boasted that he was happy in his condition, and did not intend to change it; but he was not a musty old bachelor, nor a crusty one, nor a misanthropical one; and he avowed no antipathy to the fair sex, not he; far from it, he pretended—the sly, old fox—that his admiration for the whole sex in general had been the cause of his never centering his affection on one member of it in particular.

He was quite a lady's man, was Plain Jones, and on any fine summer's day he could be seen between four and five o'clock, dressed in faultless style, with a gay little flower in his button-hole, promenading St. James' or Notre Dame Streets, bowing and smiling at his many lady acquaintances in a style which put some of the younger beaux to the blush; and he has

K

even been seen to give a sly wink as some particulaly handsome woman has passed him, and has been known to make use of such expressions as "very fine girl"—somehow he had a way of calling all women not grey-headed or ugly, "girls"—"remarkably neat figure;" "an uncommonly well-turned ankle;" "what a perfectly beautiful face," and other similar phrases which showed that he considered himself quite a judge of the various phases of female beauty. But there was nothing of the libertine about Plain Jones, and although he frequently had lady clients, young and pretty ones too, sometimes, not a name stood higher amongst the advocates, and others who did not call themselves "lawyers'—although other people did—for morality and respectability, than did his.

It was a warm day in September, about four years ago, and Plain Jones was endeavoring to keep as cool as circumstances and the weather would permit in his close, stuffy office, when there came a modest rap, as from a parasol on the antagonistic door. Now be it known that Plain Jones had two offices, an outer one into which the antagonistic door opened, and which was occupied by his two clerks and his boy; and an inner one used by himself, and in which he received his clients. On this particular September day both clerks happened to be out and the boy was left in charge of the outer office.

Jones' boy was scrubby.

It seems to me that most lawyers' boys have a tendency to scrubbiness; but Jones' boy had more than

the usual amount. He was short; but he was not fat.
Not that he had any particular disposition towards
unusual leanness, he was simply not fat; and his bones
seemed to be of that kind which develope themselves
faster than flesh could form to cover them, and gave
that general appearance known, with reference usually to horses, as "high in bone, but low in flesh."
He was not a pretty boy. His face was large
and flat; with high cheek bones, a dirty yellow-
brownish skin—sadly in need of soap and water
—a short flat nose with extravagantly wide nostrils; and a mouth capable of biting a full sized
pippin in half at one snap, a feat he was very fond of
performing when he could possess himself of the
necessary two cents. He had too many teeth, had
Jones' boy. Nature had been too bountiful to him in
this respect; teeth grew out in all sorts of unexpected
places in his mouth, and when he yawned and opened
a chasm in his head something like twelve inches in
circumference, he had the appearance of having another boy's mouth inside his with the teeth trying to
escape. His eyes were round and saucer like, of a
nondescript color; and his hair was of a brick red
hue, worn close cropped, and with a propensity to
stick up unpleasantly at the crown. But the strong
point about Jones' boy was his ears. I have heard the
terms "clam shells," "flappers," &c., applied to ears,
but in shape, size and general appearance the ears of
Jones' boy more resembled a couple of those substan-
tial articles of food known as "slap-jacks" than any-

thing else. He seemed proud of his ears too, did Jones' boy, and had a way of working them up and down, back and forth, making horrible grimaces the while, which was fearful and wonderful to see. His clothes were not new, indeed they looked as if they never had been new and were most ridiculously short at the wrists and ankles, the bottoms of his trowsers disclaiming the slightest connection with the tops of his boots and the sleeves of his jacket displaying an affection for his elbows which left several inches of remarkably dirty wristband constantly exposed to view. His wristbands were always dirty; just as his clothes seemed never to have been new, and although there is reason to believe that he sometimes changed his shirt, there was never any very perceptible change in its color, which led to the belief amongst the frequenters of the office that one of his bigger brothers wore it for a month or so first, and then transferred it to him when it had reached a stage where he could not get it much dirtier.

He was of a playful disposition, was Jones' boy. Most lawyers' boys have always appeared to me to possess playful dispositions, and give vent to it in various ways such as lolling out of windows, dropping pillets of paper on the heads of passers by; tormenting the caretaker's cat if they are so fortunate that she possesses one; whistling popular negro minstrel airs in a very loud key; practising clog dances in passages; performing daring and perilous feats on the bannisters; playing at "tag" in the corridors and on the stairs; singing little snatches of songs in very discordant tones; and in other equally pleasant ways conducting themselves in a manner calculated as much as possible to be agreeable and amusing to the busy clerks—for they generally take care to see that their employers are out before they begin to display their accomplishments—and frequently causing the sudden propulsion of a book or other missile at their heads which causes them much merriment; for they are quick dodgers, are lawyers boys, and as difficult to hit as a bat, unless you can be fortunate enough to steal on them in an unguarded moment from the rear.

Jones' boy was an adept at all these accomplishments except looking out of the window, which, occupying as he did a back office with only one window presenting a view of twenty feet of blank wall surmounted by a delapidated chimney, and the sides of two neighboring houses, he was unable to practice to any advantage. This often depressed the spirits of Jones' boy, and time frequently hung heavy on his hands when his employer was in, so he invented a new amusement to while away his spare moments. He killed flies.

Not in the usual manner with his hand or handkerchief. He was too much of a sportsman for that. He took one of the office files and sharpened the end of it to needle-like fineness; then he procured five cents worth of molasses, and pouring a little on a blotting pad he would poise his spear and wait for game. At first he used to wait for flocks and take his chance

out of the lot; but so adroit had he now become by
long practice, that he could bring down his single
fly with unerring percision, just as soon as it alighted
near the seductive but ensnaring sweet. He was very
busy on the September morning I have already referred to, and as flies were numerous was having good
sport, so that the rap previously mentioned was
thrice repeated before he condescended to take any
notice of it and cry out,

"Come in!"

Then ensued a struggle with the door, which so
much amused Jones' boy that he forsook his favorite
amusement for a while, leaving the molasses to be
devoured by the flies, and regaled himself with the
uneffectual efforts of the party outside to conquer the
antagonistic door.

"Pull it, stoopid," he said in a low voice, so that
Plain Jones in the inner office might not hear him,
"A long pull, and a strong pull and a pull altogether."

"Please open it for me," said a soft, sweet voice
outside.

"My eyes," exclaimed Jones' boy, "it's a woman,"
and he instantly dropped on his knees and applied
his eye to the keyhole. "Ain't she a pretty one,
Oh no, not at all!" he continued, as he hastily rose,
licked the palm of his hand, passed it several times
over the crown of his head to plaster down the hair
that would stand up, and lifted the latch for the lady
to enter.

A young girl, apparently not more than seventeen

or eighteen, exquisitely beautiful, with great masses of golden hair flowing loose over her shoulders, and dressed in the height of fashion, stepped into the room; and, after bestowing a glance almost of terror, at Jones' boy—who was smiling in a sweet seductive way as only a gorilla or a lawyer's boy can smile—asked,

"Is Mr. Jones in?"

"Yes'um; right in there, m'um: lady to see you, sir," he said quite briskly, showing the way and bowing politely as she passed him; but the effect was somewhat marred a moment after by his putting his thumb into one of the pits which did duty with him as nostrils, almost up to the first joint, and meditatively digging away as he walked slowly over to his desk to resume his pleasant crusade against the flies.

Plain Jones rose as the young lady entered, bowed in his politest style, smiled his blandest smile, and offered her a chair with a gallant sweep of his right arm towards it inviting her to be seated.

"Mamma asked me to give you this note and say she was too unwell to come to you herself, and would take it as a favor if you could make it convenient to call on her sometime to-day, or to-morrow; she thinks the business is important."

"Certainly, certainly, my dear, pray be seated;" somehow Plain Jones had a habit of addressing young ladies as "my dear," but he did it in a fatherly sort of way, and they did'nt seem to mind it,

"Mamma is very sorry to trouble you; but we only returned from the seaside yesterday, and mamma found a letter waiting for her which annoyed her so much she is not able to leave the hou ·day. It is too bad to have to·trouble you."

"No trouble at all, my dear; your mamma"—but then Plain Jones stopped, puzzled; for he had not opened the letter and he did not know her mamma's name. So with old fashioned politeness, which the youth of the present day don't know, or don't practice, he asked permission to break the seal; which being granted with a smile, he opened the envelope, and extracting a tiny sheet of rose colored paper, very slightly scented, read the following:—

ALASKA VILLA,
15th September, 1869.

DEAR MR. JONES,—I only returned home yesterday and my nerves are so *terribly* shaken by a *dreadful* letter I found awaiting me, that I am *utterly unable* to leave the house to-day. May I ask you as a *great favor* to call on me at your *earliest convenience*. I know I am imposing a *serious tax* on your valuable time, but the letter says the business is *very* urgent, and I must consult my lawyer *at once*, so pray forgive me.

Apologising for the inconvenience I feel I am putting you to,

Believe me, Yours sincerely,
LOUISA TRYSON.

P.S.—Tilly will show you the *horrid* letter I received.

Plain Jones sat for a moment with the letter in his hand considering, and while he is doing so I will explain who the writer of the letter was.

Mrs. Tryson was the widow of an old business friend who had died some two years ago, leaving a wife, and one child by a former marriage, and a comfortable little property of about $5,000 a year, the management of which was in Jones' hands.

Plain Jones had had very little trouble in managing the property; for it was all invested in the city and left to Mrs. Tryson entire until Tilly was twenty-one, when the estate was to be evenly divided between the two ladies. The only provisos were that, in the event of Mrs. Tryson marrying again before her stepdaughter, she should forfeit half of her portion, which then went to Jones; and should Miss Tryson marry under the age of twenty-one she forfeited half of her portion which in that event also went to Jones; with the further proviso that if Mrs. Tryson married first Tilly should not forfeit any portion of her fortune for marrying before she was twenty-one.

Now Jones was well acquainted with Mrs. Tryson, who frequently called at his office on business; but he rarely visited her; and, from the fact of Miss Tryson having been at school in England for seven or eight years past, and only returning during the present summer, Jones had not seen her since she was a little girl.

"Dear me, Miss—Miss Tilly," exclaimed Jones

after his pause," I declare I should never have recognized you. You've—you've—grown so much," he continued, quite ignoring the fact that girls usually do grow between the ages of ten and eighteen. "When I saw you last you were in short—that is, you were only so high," and he held his hand about a couple of inches above the desk to illustrate his meaning.

"Taller than that, I think," replied Tilly, smiling and displaying such pretty rows of small sparkling white teeth that Jones could not help feeling he would like her to bite him. "I know I have grown a great deal and changed very much, so I could not expect you to recognize me; but I knew you in a moment, you have'nt changed a bit,"—Jones thought she need not have said that—"unless you have been getting younger while I have been away." Jones thought that very neat of her, altho' he tried to say something about being "an old man."

"Oh, you're not an old man yet," rattled on Miss Tilly, "although I can remember you ever since I was a baby, almost"—Jones thought she was rather too fond of ancient history—"and used to toss me in your arms and ride me to Banbury Cross."—Jones thought he would like to do it now, but only smiled at the reminiscence. "You used to be a good, kind friend to me when I was a little girl, you must not be a cross old guardian to me now I am a woman; although Papa's will does not recognize me as a woman for three year's to come," she added a little petulantly.

"Oh, that is on only one point, you know; and I am sure you will not want to run away from us before then. Three years is not long to wait."

Tilly said nothing, but looked as if she thought it was altogether too long.

"I am forgetting all about mamma's commission; will you go to see her?"

"Certainly; I have an appointment at twelve, I will go immediately after that. You may say I will be there by two."

"Oh, then, if you like, I will call for you at half-past one with the carriage, and we can go up together. I have some shopping to do which will occupy me until that time."

Jones thought how pleasant it would be to enjoy a drive of a couple of miles with such a charming young creature, and consented; then he asked for the letter Mrs. Tryson referred to in her note.

Now Miss Tilly had left the letter on her dressing-table, and she knew it; but she went through a most elaborate search of her pockets and reticule, and at last, after Jones had several times assured her it was of no consequence as he could see it when he called, declared she must have left it at home.

"No matter at all, my dear, don't distress yourself about it; I daresay it is not very serious, ladies are so easily frightened by letters they do not clearly understand the meaning of."

"I know you men think women cannot understand any letters except love-letters, but I have a higher opinion of my sex than that."

"Oh, you wrong us, at least as far as I am personally concerned; although I do not deny that love-letters are very pleasant things to receive."

"Do you get many?" she asked archly, with that winning smile of hers.

"Not now, my dear. Young ladies do not think it worth while to favor an old man like me."

"Perhaps you do not try them," she retorted still in that arch manner.

"Well, to own the truth, my dear, I don't suppose I do; I have lived too long alone to think of changing my condition now, and no man has any right to pay particular attention to any lady when he has not 'serious intentions,' as the saying is."

Something very like a frown crossed Miss Tilly's face for an instant; but she chased it away with a smile and rose to go.

Jones insisted upon escorting her down stairs to the carriage, although she assured him she could find her way alone very well, or with the assistance of that "pretty" boy of his; which latter remark being overheard by Jones' boy, that young gentleman acknowledged the compliment by kissing his hand several times to her as she went down the stairs, and then turned a couple of handsprings in the passage, and stood himself up on his head in a corner in honor of the occasion,

CHAPTER II.

MRS. TRYSON.

Mrs. Tryson lived in a very pretty cottage on the mountain side, and managed to enjoy life as much as a fascinating widow of thirty-five with a comfortable jointure, and no small encumbrances possibly could. She married Tryson, who was twenty years her senior, when she was nineteen, and as none of her own children lived she had grown to look on Tilly quite as her own child and loved her quite as much as if she really had been. But Tilly as a child and Tilly as a beautiful young woman of eighteen were two very different persons, as Mrs. Tryson found when she took her step-daughter to Cacouna with her immediately after the latter's return to Canada. Miss Tilly attracted rather the lion's share of attention, and, altho' Mrs. Tryson was far from being jealous of her step-daughter, she could not avoid feeling a little pique at the sudden desertion of some of her most devoted admirers to worship at a younger and fairer shrine.

Not much fairer though, for Mrs. Tryson was as rosy cheeked, buxom, fascinating a little widow as any in the city, and more than one or two had tried to induce her to change her state, but without success. Not that Mrs. Tryson was particularly enamoured of widowhood, and intended to pass the remainder of her days in mourning; but, in the first place she had not met anyone since Tryson's death who had made any great impression on her heart; and next, she had no idea of forfeiting half her fortune by such a step as matrimony before Tilly was of the age prescribed in her father's will.

Of course, Mrs. Tryson did not think the provision of the will a wise one, which she declared "only put it into the girl's head to want to get married," but as the provision was there and could not be got over very well, she had almost reconciled herself to the idea that they must both wait three years. Mrs. Tryson was in the parlor when Jones and Tilly arrived, and looked an exceedingly interesting invalid as she lay half reclining on a sofa with a becoming morning wrapper pulled around her so as to display to advantage the general contour of a very pretty figure.

"Oh, Mr. Jones, how kind of you to come at once," she exclaimed, extending her hand, which was particularly small and soft, as Plain Jones advanced towards her. "I would never have troubled you only that letter frightened me so. What do you think of the dreadful business?"

"Well,—really—humph! The fact is, Miss Tilly forgot to take it with her and I have not seen it yet; but do not let it annoy you, it cannot be very serious."

"Oh, but it is dreadful. It threatens to deprive me of all my property; to turn me out of house and home. What shall I do. You'll help me, Mr. Jones, won't you?" and in her excitement she extended both hands towards him in an imploring way.

"Certainly, certainly," said Jones; taking the extended hands and pressing them gently—I said they were soft hands and pleasant to squeeze. "You are exciting yourself unnecessarily, where is this terrible letter?"

"Here it is," said Tilly, who had entered the room just in time to see Jones take Mrs. Tryson's hands; but, of course, she did not notice the squeeze.

"Now let me see what this wonderful document amounts to," said Plain Jones, spreading the letter open, and placing a gold double eyeglass on his nose; for Jones used glasses, occasionally, not altogether because he needed them, but partly because he looked well in them; and then, everybody will admit that a lawyer looks more imposing with a formidable pair of double eyeglasses astraddle of his nose than without them.

Plain Jones adjusted his glasses, and read:

Montreal, 12th September, 1869.

MADAM,

I am instructed by my client S. C. Tryson, Esq., to enter suit against you for the recovery of the property now illegally in your possession, under a, so-called, will of your late husband; and have to request that you will favor me with the address of your solicitor, at your earliest convenience, that I may consult with him. Mr. Tryson claims to be the eldest son of your late husband by a marriage contracted prior to his acquaintance with you; I regret to say that his claims appear to be exceedingly well founded and would advise you to lose no time in consulting your solicitor.

   Madam,
    I have the honor to be
    Your very obedient servant,
       PETER SNAP,
        Solicitor.

To Mrs. L. Tryson.

Mrs. Tryson watched Jones closely while he read the letter, and her fears were not at all allayed by the look of astonishment which crept over his face as he read. Tilly turned to the window so that her own face was partly in the shade and she could watch the others unobserved.

"When did you get this letter?" asked Jones when he had finished reading it.

"I found it here when I came home yesterday. Oh, Mr. Jones, isn't it terrible? And to think that James should have—"

"It's all nonsense," cried Plain Jones quite hotly, "this letter was never written by a lawyer. There is no such solicitor in Montreal as Peter Snap. There never was a lawyer called Snap, except in *Ten Thousand a Year*, and that's all gammon. My dear madam, this is some miserable hoax some unprincipled scamp has had the audacity to perpetrate on you. The rascal; I'll find him out and teach him what it is to send threatening letters to a lady;" and Jones became quite excited and gave the letter a vicious sort of slap as if he wished it was somebody's head.

"Not true! a hoax! Oh, Mr. Jones, are you quite sure?" and the small, white hands were again impulsively extended; and again Plain Jones took them in his and pressed them gently.

"Perfectly certain. It is the work of some villain who has been trying to frighten you."

"I am afraid he succeeded then," said the widow, trembling violently, and looking very much as if she would like to put her head on Jones' shoulder and have a good cry; but just then a little sound came from Tilly, which sounded half like an hysterical sob, and half like a suppressed laugh, which made them both start; and Mrs. Tryson resumed her seat on the sofa, while Plain Jones returned his gold eyeglasses to the pocket in which he usually carried them, and turned to Tilly who advanced towards him.

"A hoax!" exclaimed that young lady, "who could have been so wicked?"

Ah! That was the question. Who could have been so wicked? The three sat near together and discussed this curious letter. Who could have written it? What was the object? What did it mean?

"Are you quite sure, Mr. Jones," said Mrs. Tryson, "that James,—"

L

"Nonsense, my dear madam, nonsense. I knew James Tryson from boyhood. He was married, as you know, before he met you; but as for his entering into any clandestine marriage before that, it is ridiculous. I knew the man too well for that; it was not the sort of man to trifle with solemn matters."

"But that man says he is heir at-law?"

"Heir at fiddlesticks, ma'am! What is the good of his being heir-at-law when we have an incontestible will to fall back on."

"Does that make any difference?" asked Tilly, quite innocently.

"All the difference in the world, my dear," replied Plain Jones, rising to go.

"Won't you stay and take lunch, Mr. Jones?" asked Mrs. Tryson, hospitably, "I have unintentionally spoiled your own lunch, stay and share ours;" and she accompanied the invitation with a winning smile which quite captived at Jones.

Tilly turned away again, and there was no doubt this time that she laughed, but very softly to herself.

Jones hesitated. Some wise man has said, "who hesitates is lost," and as far as there could be said to be any winning or losing in this case, Jones' hesitation was certainly fatal to him, for at that moment the servant entered and announced lunch, and Jones consented to remain.

Now, altho' Jones had occasionally called on Mrs. Tryson during her widowhood on matters of business, he had never partaken of a meal in the house since his old friend died, and, even during his lifetime, Jones had only dined with him occasionally on special occasions, for their intimacy was more of a business than a social nature, and he was agreeably surprised to find the widow's taste so nearly agreed with his own.

The lunch was a light one; a cold duck; a cool, refreshing salad; a fruit stand filled with grapes, peaches, &c.; a tart and a bottle of sherry comprised its main features; and if Jones had been requested to order a lunch exactly to his taste he could not have suited himself better; for Jones was something of an epicure in his way and liked good living. He strongly maintained, however, that dining in the middle of the day was a barbarity, and could on no account have been induced to partake of a hearty meal later than breakfast, until his own proper dinner hour at six; the widow's lunch was, therefore, just the thing to suit Jones. Still there was a drawback; no earthly happiness can be perfect and a sudden damper was put on Jones' pleasure by a thought which crossed his mind.

He would have to carve the duck.

Carving is one of the lost arts; and Jones' education had been sadly neglected in this particular branch. He had no more idea of the anatomy of a duck than a a duck had of his; what little carving he had been obliged to do, he had always done on general principles; he would place the fork firmly in the most available spot of the bird to be carved, and hew and hack about until, by main strength, he had reduced it to a mass of mangled remains. He knew that by great exertion he could tear the toughest chicken, or the most ancient duck to pieces, and even come off partially successful after an encounter with an obstinate old goose; but his carving never satisfied him, it was one of the few things he did that he did badly; and he sighed gently as he took his seat at the little round table on which the repast was spread.

But the widow soon put him at his ease by insisting on carving the duck herself, altho' Jones made a desperate effort to appear very anxious to save her the trouble. The widow was obstinate. She was one of those few women who really carve well, and at small parties in her own house she was fond of displaying her accomplishment.

Carving is like everything else, very easy when you know how. The widow knew how; and Jones sat in silent admiration, watching her, as she pulled her loose sleeves out of the way, thereby displaying part of a very plump, white forearm; gently impaled the duck with the fork and gracefully and dexterously carved it. It looked like magic the way the legs, wings, side-bones, breast, neck-bone, and merry-thought came apart as the fair white hands fluttered for an instant over them; and as Jones gazed in wonder he felt that he almost wished he was a duck to be

so quickly and scientifically dissected by those fair,
hands. But I fear if Jones had been a duck he would
have proved rather a tough one.

Now there was nothing in the fact of Mrs. Tryson's
carving a duck to cause laughter, nor in any way to
account for the merry little peal which suddenly
burst from Tilly's lips; nor was there any apparent
cause for her blushing so vividly and hiding her face
in her handkerchief and declaring that "something
tickled her." Yet she did it; and several times during
the meal some amusing thought seemed to recur to
her, and she appeared on the point of laughing out
again.

A round table is *par excellence* the table for a small
party; everything is within easy reach so that very
little waiting on is needed; and everybody is within
sight and hearing of everybody else. It is certainly
conducive to jollity and our little party of three
were very merry, especially Tilly, who was the mer-
riest of the three, and laughed longest and loudest at
some of Plain Jones' jokes, for he could joke could
Plain Jones, and tell very good stories too when he
pleased, and to use a common expression, "he
came out strong" on this occasion, and kept his
two fair auditors thoroughly amused. Mrs. Tryson
had recovered her health and spirits wonderfully after
the sudden disposal of the threatening letter by
Plain Jones, and now appeared as the merry, jovial
little soul she usually was.

After lunch they returned to the parlor, and, Mrs. Tryson having excused herself for a few minutes, Tilly played some selections from Offenbach, and sang a merry little French song, in a style which perfectly charmed Plain Jones, who was a great lover of music, and in his enthusiasm he made a confession which he rarely made.

He admitted that he performed on the violin. "Only a little," he said modestly; but Tilly went into ecstacies, and engaged him in such a lively conversation on musical matters until Mrs. Tryson's return, that Plain Jones had no opportunity of suggesting the propriety of retiring, which he had for some time been meditating.

"Oh, mamma!" exclaimed Tilly, enthusiastically as Mrs. Tryson entered." Only think, Mr. Jones plays the fiddle!" but, seeing a slight shade pass over the usually serene face of Jones, she colored up and the next time she mentioned that noble instrument she did not forget to call it a violin.

"Does he! how nice; why you can play duetts together; if Mr. Jones will take pity on two lone women and spend an evening with us," she added with a smile.

Of course, Jones could only expre the pleasure it would give him; and made a general statement about "some evening," but Tilly immediately cut in:

"Come next Thursday," she said," and be sure to bring *the violin*."

Plain Jones promised he would come and went away smiling.

Now there was nothing particularly strange or amusing, in Mrs. Tryson's inviting an old friend and legal adviser to spend an evening at her house; but it appeared to act with wonderful force on Miss Tilly's risibilities; for as soon as Jones had gone she ran up to her own room, locked the door, threw herself on the sofa and laughed until she seemed to be going into hysterics; then she danced about the room like a mad thing, singing and laughing; and every now and then crying out "Oh, its too good," "Oh, its too funny," and then she sat down and wrote a long letter beginning, "My dearest, dearest darling" and ending—well never mind the ending we haven't quite got to that yet.

Plain Jones drove away—for Mrs. Tryson insisted on his taking the carriage—in the most enjoyable frame of mind he had been in for some time; and he frequently confessed to himself that he had seldom spent so pleasant an afternoon. But the prominent idea in his mind seemed to be Tilly's growth, and several times he repeated to himself, "how she has grown;" as if the fact of her having changed from girlhood to womanhood in eight years, was quite a remarkable one, and evinced an unusual degree of smartness on her part. And by and by his thoughts changed a little in form, and he added to his thought, "and what a nice girl she is," and in this frame of mind he reached his office.

Jones' boy had had a happy afternoon in his master's absence, and in the various developments of his happiness had been twice kicked, once cuffed on the ear until he bellowed again, and at last summarily ejected from the office by the two clerks who had been trying hard to copy some deeds. He was just amusing himself singing " Good bye, Charlie" through the keyhole for the benefit of the clerks inside when Jones returned; that brought him to his senses in a moment and he announced quickly, " Mr. Chops has been waiting for you for over an hour, sir, and he says he will call again to-morrow as he couldn't wait no longer."

" Bless me!" exclaimed Jones, consulting his watch, " half-past four, and I promised to cook up Chops' case for him at three; dear, dear, what a pleasant afternoon I must have spent, that I never once thought of Chops," and he passed into the office.

But Jones' boy did not immediately follow his master. He stood watching his retreating figure until the door was closed; then he shook his head in a deprecatory manner as if he wished it to be distinctly understood that he highly disapproved of Jones' conduct; and he solemnly shook his finger in a menacing way as if to warn Jones that he really would not be able to overlook such gross inattention to business. Then a brilliant idea seemed to occur to him. He smartened himself up a bit; smiled that bewitching smile of his; went through a pantomime of gracefully tucking a lady's arm under his, and bending low as if whispering soft nothings to his imaginary companion, proudly promenaded the passage-way for the next five minutes. What his exact thoughts were I am unable to say; but I have reason to believe he was imitating what he supposed Jones had been doing when he ought to have been attending to the case of Chops.

CHAPTER III.

MR. STEDMAN.

PLAIN JONES kept his appointment for Thursday evening, and took his violin with him. He was a mild and inoffensive performer on that noble instrument, and scraped up and down in a very correctly mechanical sort of way, throwing no feeling whatever into his playing. Just as I have heard some young ladies, with good voices, sing "Home, Sweet Home," or *Ah, che la Morte*, or some other equally touching melody with an almost painfully mechanical and mathematical correctness, but without one atom of feeling. The fact is, Jones had a superabundance of music in his soul, but he could not succeed in drawing much of it out of his violin.

Still Tilly was greatly charmed with his playing and the widow said it was " sweet," and they managed to get up some very pleasant little musical parties to themselves. Tilly's singing was far above the average, and the widow had a rich, sweet contralto which harmonised with Tilly's soprano as well as any two women's voices can harmonize; so they sang duets with violin and piano accompanyment, and Jones even tried once to take the bass, but his chin was so firmly closed on the tail piece of the violin that he breathed most of it through the openings in the sound-board into the body of the violin and the effect was not harmonious. He did not try it again.

Of course, it must be understood that the first visit was only the forerunner of many others, and indeed it soon began to be looked on as a settled thing that Jones should spend at least one evening a week at Alaska Villa; and although he did not, as the saying is, "hang up his hat in the hall," he certainly did his violin case and left it there.

Nor was music the only amusement. Tilly soon discovered that amongst his various accomplishments Plain Jones could play chess, and as she was a fair player she at once challenged him, and they had several pleasant games together. But Tilly quickly admitted that she was no match for Plain Jones and handed him over to her step-mother who was a much better player, and he and the widow had many mimic battles with varying success; for the widow was skilful in attack and Plain Jones was often hard pressed to prevent a quick and disgraceful checkmate. Tilly would sit by and look on, but after a little while she usually strayed off to the piano and played and sung softly to herself, or brought out her writing desk and began another letter to "my dearest, &c.": it was surprising what an extensive correspondence this young lady had just about this time. It was noticeable, however, that Jones' attention was always distracted from his game when Tilly was not near; and he always endeavoured to avoid chess and substitute music so that they could all be together. But Tilly was obstinate and managed in some way or other to contrive that he should have his dose of chess very nearly as regularly as his music.

Very quiet and happy were those evenings at Alaska Villa, and Plain Jones began to find a home like feeling come over him there, which he had not experienced since he was a boy. The change in his feeling was very gradual, and the Fall had slipped away and Christmas was close at hand before Jones himself began to be at all conscious that any feeling stronger than that of pleasnre at being in the company of his old friend's widow and daughter, had anything to do with his visits at Alaska Villa.

But it was not at Alaska Villa alone that Plain Jones met the Trysons. They had many mutual friends, and he frequently encountered them at their houses. On these occasions Plain Jones balanced his attentions so nicely between mother and daughter that no one could say he was paying particular attention to either; only, he generally managed to escort Tilly to the carriage, greatly to the chagrin of many spiring yonths, who petulantly observed to each other, " Why don't the old fool stick to the widow?"

Nor was it at friends' houses only that they met either; for Tilly took a great passion for the theatre, and became a great patroness of that noble old barn in Cotté street; and it so happened that she usually managed so that Jones either accompanied them, or came into their box during the performance. For Jones was quite a patron of the drama, and sat out the very mediocre entertainment given, with a perseverance worthy of a better cause. Tilly too always evinced great interest in the play, and usually insisted on staying until the finish; but the widow was sometimes a little bored, and yawned slightly behind her fan.

Now it happened, quite by accident, that on the first occasion of their visiting the theatre, a young man, with whom Jones was well acquainted, chanced to be standing in the lobby of the dress circle, and, not noticing that Jones had ladies with him, stopped him to say "good evening"; this caused the whole party to halt for an instant, and that instant sufficed for Mrs. Tyson to recognize in the young gentleman a Cacouna acqaintance who had been very attentive to both Tilly and herself during the past summer.

"Oh, Mr. Stedman! How have you been since you left Cacouna?"

"Quite well, thanks. You and Miss Tryson have been quite well, I hope."

"Quite, thanks. Shall we see you in the box by and by?"

"Yes, with pleasure."

And so Mr. Stedman "dropped in" for a few minutes, and his few minutes proved to be pretty long ones, for they lasted until the end of the second act; and after that, Mr. Stedman managed, by accident, to be at the theatre every evening that Mrs. Tryson was, and, of course, he always dropped into her box for a few minutes; he seemed to be a lucky fellow, too, for it happened, by chance of course, that on the evenings he did not go to the theatre Mrs. Tryson was not there.

He was a very nice young fellow, Mr. Henry Stedman, and Jones, who knew his family well, spoke very highly of him. He was very attentive to Mrs. Tryson, and very polite to Tilly; and, after a while, the former invited him to visit her at Alaska Villa. After that the trio became a quartette, and Mr. Stedman was soon very nearly as constant a visitor at the villa as Jones.

The amusements became a little more regular after Stedman's appearance; for Jones almost always paired off with Tilly at the piano, and Stedman played chess with the widow.

The only one of the quartette who did not seem perfectly satisfied with this new arrangement was Tilly; and she made several attempts to get Jones back to chess with the widow, but met with but little success, as Jones did not second her efforts very warmly, and Stedman showed pretty plainly that he did not intend to be robbed of his pleasant little *tete-a-tetes* with the widow across the chess table; so Tilly had no recourse but to confide in her " dearest, dearest, &c.," which she did at considerable length.

Then Tilly changed her tactics a little, and visited Jones frequently at his office, sometimes inducing him to go out driving with her step-mother and herself. At first Jones felt a little delicacy about driving out with the ladies, but he soon got over that, and Miss Tilly congratulated herself that she had outgeneralled Mr. Stedman. Not too fast, Miss Tilly; perhaps you have not taken the whole game into account.

Now Tilly's visits to Jones' office had an effect of which that young lady little dreamed.

Jones' boy fell in love with her.

It must be borne in mind that Jones' boy was about twelve years old, a very susceptible age; that he was scrubby, a state which tends to precocity; and that he was red-headed, and it is generally said—for what reason, or on what grounds I do not know—that persons having red hair are more easily overcome by the God of Love than those who boast of hair of any other hue. It was about the third or fourth visit of Tilly's to the office when this passion of Jones' boy first showed itself in visible form; but the first sign was a tremendous one;

He put on a clean shirt.

Never before had Jones' boy been known to commit such an act, and his appearance at the office created quite a sensation; but he cared nothing for that; he waited anxiously for *her*, and when she came he threw open his waistcoat in a careless sort of way and smiled so markedly that you could not only see all his teeth, but nearly half way down his throat. But she was in a hurry that day and passed him without looking at him. Then the heart of Jones' boy sank within him, and in the extreme bitterness of his spirit he speared every unfortunate fly which made its appearance in the office that day.

But the heart of youth is buoyant, and by the next morning Jones' boy was himself again, and had hit on a new idea. He washed himself perfectly clean for the first time in many months, and invested all his capital in a pot of Castor oil pomatum, which he had heard somebody say would turn red hair black; but the only effect produced by that was that the chief clerk, who had a particular antipathy to the smell of Castor oil, forcibly carried him to the nearest barber's shop and had him shampooed, an operation which Jones' boy did not at all relish; for, never having been shampooed before, he kept his eyes open when the water was turned on his head and both eyes got pretty well filled with soap suds. A day or two elapsed before he could pick up courage for another attempt to attract Tilly's attention; but when he did it was a great one.

He got a new suit of clothes.

You must not suppose that Jones' boy had the clothes made to order. Not at all. After a desperate effort he induced his mother to give him three dollars, and with that he purchased an entire suit from a

pawnbroker—who had advanced fifty cents on them
—and felt happy. Now, all the clothes Jones' boy
had ever worn before were manifestly two small for
him; this suit was just as palpably too large. The
trousers were so long that he had to turn up about
eight inches at the bottoms, and the jacket was so full
that he could easily have carried a week's provisions
in it without inconvenience. The chief clerk declared
it "a good deal of a fit," and he probably was right.
But Jones' boy cared little for the remarks of jealous
clerks—he was sure they were jealous of his good
looks—and having washed his face again and reck.
lessly put on another clean shirt, impatiently waited
Tilly's arrival.

She came; and the moment she saw him a peal of
silvery laughter rang out such as that dingy old building had seldom heard within its walls; and when he
grinned in delight, she almost went into hysterics and
ran into Jones' office to ask who that funny boy was.
Jones' boy heard her and his heart grew so big in his
bosom that he was forced to go down to the street
door and give vent to his feelings; which he did by
whistling "Rule Brittania" in so loud and shrill a key
that an excitable horse across the street ran away,
smashed the carriage he was attached to all to pieces
against a lamp post, and so furnished an item for the
evening papers.

After this little episode the current of Jones' boy's
love took another turn. The summer was quite gone

M

now and with it the flies, and he found it difficult to
amuse himself while Jones was in the office; so he
became epistolatory, and used to amuse himself
writing love-letters to Tilly, which he never delivered. He even went so far as to endeavor to soar
forth in poetry, and after a whole afternoon spent in
the throes of composition he produced the following:
          butiFul gurl of mI sole
          smile oN the 1 who Adoors the
But there his muse suddenly deserted him, and no
amount of persuasion could induce her to return. Not
being able to succeed at poetry, he next tried his
hand at art and spoiled all the paper he could get from
the clerks, endeavoring to draw Tilly's likeness.

This passion of Jones' boy was innocently fed by
Tilly, who would sometimes say a few kind words to
him if Jones happened to be out when she called; and
this little encouragement so elated Jones' boy that he
began to argue to himself that Tilly did not come to
the office really to see Jones, but to see him. Then
he determined to make known his passion, and in
order that he might gain all the advantage which his
most imposing appearance could give him, he plastered
his head again with the Castor oil pomatum which led
to his expulsion from the office by the chief clerk the
moment he made his appearance.

This occurred just a week before Christmas. The
snow was down, winter fairly closed in, and Jones'
boy, expelled from the office on account of the un-

pleasant odor of his head, found refuge in the lower hall-way, and amused himself peeping through one of the little side windows at the sleighs going by. He had not been at his post more than five minutes when a covered sleigh with a lady and gentleman in it drew up at a short distance from the office, and before the lady alighted Jones' boy distinctly saw the gentleman kiss her and she seemed to like it too.

The lady was Tilly.

To say that the hair of Jones' boy's head stood on end would be to state an inaccuracy, it was too tightly plastered down with Castor oil pomatum for that; but it made the best effort it could to rise, and deadly and dangerous thoughts darkly flitted across his mind. Oh, that he had now the spear in his hand with which he has been used to impale flies, how gladly he would have plunged it into the heart of that base miscreant who had dared to press the lips of his beloved! And to think of her, the deceitful thing, coming to the office to see him and allowing another to kiss her on the way, when even he had never dared to take such a liberty! It was terrible to think of; and in his jealous rage Jones' boy scowled darkly at Tilly as she passed him at the door, which made her laugh even more than his smile had frightened her; for as his smile was terrible so his scowl was irresistibly funny.

That smile decided Jones' boy on a scheme of vengeance. He determined that if he could not have Tilly himself that black-moustached stranger should not have her, so he went to his desk and penned the following unique note to Jones:

Thare is a feLla makin luv tu yur ɢurl i seed him ᴋiss er luᴋ out

a Fren

This epistle he addressed to Jones at his private residence, stamped it with an office stamp and posted it with his own hand while Tilly was talking to Jones in the inner office.

Now a little change had taken place in the arrangement of the quartette of late, and the change was owing to the widow's suddenly and unexpectedly giving the cold shoulder to Stedman and bestowing all her blandishments on Jones. Neither Tilly nor Stedman seemed to object very much to being thrown more together; but Jones scarcely appeared to relish the arrangement as much as when he was more in Tilly's society.

So matters stood on the day when Jones' boy wrote his anonymous note to Jones.

On that same evening Jones received the note and it angered him more than such a trifle ought to have angered a staid, middle aged bachelor. He fumed over it, and delayed himself dressing to think of it; and the more he thought of it the more it seemed to annoy him. At last, his mind was made up and he hastily finished dressing for the party he was going to, and where he expected to meet Mrs. Tryson and Tilly. All that evening he devoted himself to Tilly, so that the widow was quite tiffed, and when he asked permission to call on her next morning, she answered rather pettishly, which somewhat surprised Jones.

Jones handed Tilly to the carriage, as usual; and as he stood for a moment on the door step he overheard young Trimmins say to Potts:

"What does old Jones run after that girl so for, if he wants to marry her why don't he do it, I'm sure he is old enough; and if he don't mean to marry her he has no business to pay her so much attention."

"Of course not," replied Potts, "confounded selfish, he can't marry them both; he ought to stick to the widow and give us young men a chance at the girl."

"Certainly," responded Trimmins.

Jones said nothing, but walked thoughtfully away; and as he drew on his overcoat he murmured to himself,

"I'll do it to-morrow."

CHAPTER IV.

HOW IT ENDED.

Jones dressed himself with more than usual care next morning, and appeared at the office in all the glory of a white waistcoat, although it was nearly mid winter. Jones had great confidence in white waistcoats; he said there was " a finish" about them which no other style of waistcoat possessed, and he always wore one on important occasions.

Jones' boy was fairly overpowered by his appearance, and immediately drew a caricature of him, adopting the easy plan of displaying the white waistcoat to proper advantage by filling up all the rest of the figure with ink.

Jones sat for a while in his office and seriously thought over the step he was about to take. The anonymous letter he had received, and the words he had overheard on the previous evening had decided him. A great change had come over him since his visits to Alaska Villa commenced. The glimpses of domestic happiness which had been disclosed to him had entirely changed his views, and he now began to think he had made a mistake in not marrying earlier in life.

Was it too late?

Jones had asked himself this question several times, but had not arrived at a satisfactory answer. The conversation he had overheard had raised a new question in his mind. Had he been too particular in his attentions to one of these ladies? Had he gone beyond the bounds of friendship and led others to suppose that he had other intentions? Jones asked himself these questions, and his conscience did not qu'te acquit him. Then Jones asked himself: Shall I get married? and his conscience answered, yes.

Then Jones put on his overcoat and gloves, pulled his cap well down over his ears, and started for Alaska Villa.

Mrs. Tryson had not passed a very happy night; in fact that estimable little widow had not been in quite as good spirits as usual for some days past. She had made a discovery. She had found out that she was not quite as contented in her present condition as she had thought she was. The widow was past the age of girlish sentimentality, and was not likely to be caught merely by a good figure or a handsome face. The three months that she had been thrown into frequent association with Jones had given her an opportunity of studying his character, and the more she studied him the more she found to admire in him; in a word the widow discovered that she cared more about Jones than she would have liked to confess without a proposal from him; and, therefore, his sudden devotion to Tilly the previous evening, and consequent neglect of her had somewhat nettled her, and caused her to answer petulantly when he had asked permission to call on her.

But the morning brought with it cooler reflection; and calm consideration told her that it must be something of importance which Jones wished to speak to her about, or why should he make a special appointment when he had been in her company all the evening and could easily have spoken to her then about any ordinary business.

Could he intend to propose?

The thought made the widow blush a little, and she glanced anxiously in the glass several times while she was dressing, to be sure that she was looking well; and she dressed with more than usual care, so that she should look as attractive as possible.

And very pretty and charming she did look as Jones entered the room and advanced towards her; and Jones evidently thought so as he took her hand, for he looked admiringly at her, and bowed with even more than his usual *empressement*.

"It is very kind of you to admit me at such an unusual hour," began Jones, in the manner of a man who has learned a speech by heart and means to say it before he can possibly forget it; "and nothing but the importance of what I have to say could have induced me to intrude on you at such an hour."

The widow interrupted him with an assurance that she was always charmed to see him at any time; but instead of putting him at his ease this assurance seemed to confuse him, for he appeared to have forgotten the connecting link in his speech and to be unable to proceed.

"You cannot be surprised, after what I have said," continued Jones, getting into the middle of his speech and forgetting that he had said nothing yet, "that I should have become weary of my present mode of life." The widow said nothing, but discreetly turned her head away, leaving her hand, however, lying carelessly on her lap so that Jones could take it easily if he felt so disposed.

"It is rather late in life, perhaps," he went on, "for me to think of matrimony; but I am not a very old man—"

"Oh, certainly not," breathed the widow in a scarcely audible voice.

"And you know the common saying, 'It is better to be an old man's darling than a young man's slave.'"

The widow did not exactly see the point of this argument, and therefore contented herself with a non-committal sigh.

"I can scarcely expect a very warm affection at my time of life," continued Jones, gently taking the hand which lay so invitingly before him in his, "but I flatter myself that I can command that feeling of respect which is often more lasting, and more conducive to true happiness than a mere girlish passion for a man of fewer years than myself."

The widow gave the slightest nod of assent and turned the least bit toward him.

"It is curious," continued Jones, abstractedly squeezing the hand he held in his, "but I have sometimes thought that this was what my old friend intended when he put that curious provision in his will."

The widow bowed her head in acknowledgement that the same thought had occurred to her.

"For in this case the forfeiture will be a mere nominal one."

Again the widow bowed in assent, and a thought crossed her mind that he was rather longer in coming to the point than there was any necessity for.

"The arrangement will not be distateful to you, I hope?" continued Jones insinuatingly, with another little pressure of the hand he held.

The widow sighed gently, and faintly articulated "No."

"And I may count on your consent?"

"Yes."

"Why then," said Jones, we may consider it settled."

"Yes," returned the widow, speaking very low and turning on him a face radiant with happiness and covered with blushes.

Jones was a little astonished at this, but he went on apparently unmoved," I am more than ever convinced I am following out the wishes of my old friend in this matter; and certain remarks I overheard last night have decided me in the opinion that it is time Tilly should have a male protector; and if her affections are not already engaged—"

"Tilly!" interrupted the widow, "What has she to do with it?"

"Why, as the person most interested, her inclinations must certainly be consulted. I shall see her at once and——"

But Jones did not finish that sentence; for the widow suddenly withdrew her hand from his and turning on him a look in which rage, contempt, surprise and shame were curiously blended, left the room without a word, her handkerchief going quickly to her eyes as she got near the door.

Jones could not understand this strange conduct, and severely blamed himself for forgetting his prepared speech and precipitating the matter so, "I was too sudden in my announcement," he thought, "the prospect of losing her step-daughter so unexpectedly has overpowered her; I will await her return."

A full half hour did Jones wait but the widow did not return, so at last he grew impatient and ringing the bell sent a servant to enquire whether Mrs. Tryson would see him again before he left. The servant soon returned with a message that his mistress was suddenly indisposed and would be unable to return, and handed him a note which Jones opened in some surprise and read as follows:

DEAR SIR,

If you think it wise and expedient at your time of life to marry a girl young enough to be your daughter, and the young lady is willing, I have no opposition to offer.

Yours truly,
LOUISA TRYSON,

It struck Jones that the consent was not couched in very flattering terms, but he did not pause to consider that and at once asked for Tilly.

"Miss Tryson went out about an hour ago, sir, and said she would not return until lunch time," replied the servant.

As it wanted two good hours to that time Jones left a message for Tilly that he would call in the evening and returned to his office.

On his way to the office Jones seriously thought of the events of the morning, and finally decided that he would make his proposal to Tilly by letter, as he felt confident he could acquit himself better on paper than if he urged his suit verbally; he, therefore, set himself to his task as soon as he reached his desk; but had only written the words "my dear" when there was a little struggle with the antagonistic door, and Tilly herself entered his room looking quite flushed and excited.

"Oh, Mr. Jones," she said before he could utter a

word, "I have been here once already this morning and you were out; I want to ask you," but then her eloquence suddenly deserted her and she became quite confused.

"I am very sorry Miss Tilly, that we chanced to miss each other, for I desired to see you this morning and have just returned from your house."

"Wanted to see me?" she exclaimed, turning pale for an instant and then flushing up again, "That is singular. What is it about?" Instead of answering, Jones rose and went to the door of the private office to see that it was properly closed, and it was only by the exercise of the greatest agility that Jones' boy escaped from the key-hole in time to avoid detection and seated himself at his desk where Jones found him industriously engaged in sticking an office file into a piece of paper. Little did Jones imagine that that paper bore a caricature of himself in his white vest and that the boy was engaged in imagination in stabbing him to the heart with the file with which he had formerly imolated flies.

Having satisfied himself that the door was closed and that they were safe from intrusion, Jones returned to his seat and asked what Tilly desired to see him about.

"Oh nothing—that is nothing important," said Tilly a little nervously. "Tell me what you wanted to see me about that was of so much consequence."

Thus urged, Jones in brief terms made a formal

proposal for her hand. It must be confessed that he did it more in a fatherly than a lover-like way; he made no great protestations of affection, but merely said that in his opinion it was time she ought to be married; that if she married anyone but him for three years to come she would forfeit half her fortune to him, and that altho' should that happen he had intended to restore it to her in his will, yet he felt he would not be carrying out her father's wishes if he did not claim it during his own lifetime; then he alluded to the impression on his mind that this was just what her father intended by the curious provision in his will, and concluded with the usual promise that he would devote his life to her happiness.

Long before he had finished Tilly was hiding her face in her hands, crying softly; and Jones' boy, who had again applied his eye to the keyhole, but could hear nothing, was shaking his fist in impotent rage at his master—who he felt assured was scolding Tilly—in fancied security, the door being between them. But alas for the vanity of human expectations! The chief clerk, returning unexpectedly at this moment, caught him by the collar, conducted him to the door, and without further ceremony, kicked him down stairs.

Tilly recovered herself a little as soon as Jones ceased speaking, and half sobbed out:

"You don't—mean to say—you want to—marry—me!"

"That is what I proposed, my dear," said Jones, soothingly.

"You ought to be ashamed of yourself," she said, so suddenly and unexpectedly that Jones involuntarily started; "No, no! I don't mean that. Oh, Mr.—Jones," with another burst of tears, "what made you—think—of—such—a—thing? I don't want to get married." Then, after a little pause, during which Jones looked on in too much astonishment to interrupt, "Just as I thought—everything was so nicely arranged, too"—more sobs—"and I'm sure mamma expected it, too," Jones started at this; "and I'm sure Harry did," Jones started still more when he heard this announcement, "and all my fine plot—gone—for—nothing," and another burst of tears closed this very intelligible speech.

Jones sat and looked at her in a state of astonishment he had rarely experienced in his legal career; and it somehow occurred to him that he did not understand the female sex quite so well as he had always prided himself he did.

Now, you must remember that Jones was not violently in love with Tilly; it was a mild sort of determination on his part, arrived at from a sudden conclusion that he was not happy as a bachelor; and his selection of Tilly as the object of his affection was as much due to what he had overheard young Trimmins and Potts say, and to what he considered the intention of Tryson's will, as anything else; therefore, although he was somewhat astonished at Tilly's sudden outburst, and naturally felt a little chagrin at his rejection, he felt none of the " pangs of rejected love" which all authors are in duty bound to describe as so terrible.

In fact, I am rather inclined to think that Jones, after the first moment of surprise, was rather relieved than otherwise, and was disposed to be as kind as possible to Tilly in her apparent distress.

"Come, come, Miss Tilly, he said, kindly patting her on the head, " don't cry so; this is only a foolish fancy of a stupid old man, and I will soon get over it. Believe me, child, that the silly notion I had will make no difference in my feeling towards you. I should probably make a very poor husband for a lively young girl like you, and I was a fool ever to think of it; come, let me be a good friend to you instead. Judging from your manner I should say you have some little trouble of your own, tell me what it is, and let me see if I can help you."

He said this in so kind and fatherly a manner that Tilly just threw her arms around his neck and gave him a sounding kiss without any more ado, which proceeding so astonished Jones that he quietly submitted to be kissed without offering any resistance; and Jones' boy, who had returned to his desk, and who heard the sound, was so exasperated that he made a violent stab at the ink bottle, broke it, and was for the next few minutes busily engaged wiping up ink from the desk, papers and floor with the blotting pad, which proceeding quickly obliterated all traces of the caricature of Jones, white waistcoat included.

".Oh, you good, dear, kind, darling, old guardy," exclaimed Tilly, accompanying each adjective with a kiss, "Now I can love you ever so much again."

"Yes, yes, certainly," said Jones, somewhat embarrassed; "but what did you want to consult me about?"

It was Tilly's turn to be confused now.

"I thought," she stammered, "that you—that is mamma—and Harry said—I mean if she—" and then she stopped short and looked at Jones so helplessly that he could not refrain from smiling goodhumoredly.

"Oh, ho!" he said with a rouguish twinkle in his eye, "Harry is it; I begin to think your objections to matrimony are more to the object than to the state. Come, tell me who Harry is!"

"Oh, you know him," replied Tilly blushing violently, "Mr. Stedman."

"Phew!" whistled Jones in such a loud key that the boy in the next room, who was industriously swabbing up ink, involuntarily started, and in so doing overturned a chair, which attracted Jones' attention to him and caused him to order the boy to go to dinner and bolt the outer door after him to prevent his return.

N

**IMAGE EVALUATION
TEST TARGET (MT-3)**

Photographic
Sciences
Corporation

23 WEST MAIN STREET
WEBSTER, N.Y. 14580
(716) 872-4503

"Mr. Stedman, eh!" said Jones, again taking his seat by Tilly. "You sly puss; why I thought—" but he did not say what he thought, but stopped suddenly and looked very hard at the carpet as a new idea seemed to occur to him.

"Yes," said Tilly, interrupting what he thought, "I know; but you are wrong. I told Harry he would overdo it and spoil everything."

"Spoil what!"

"Why—why—our little plot."

"Your little plot; what was that ?!"

Instead of answering directly, Tilly slipped off her chair and knelt on one knee by Jones' side, with one arm thrown over his shoulder and her face resting on the white waistcoat, so that he could not see it. Then she began to take all the starch out of that vest by crying on it, and it was a little while before Jones could get her to compose herself and answer his question. Then she said,

"Don't be angry with me—Harry and I loved each other so much—and that will made me lose half my fortune if I married for three years—unless mamma—and if she married you—fortune would remain—and so I got Harry to write that letter—and I brought you together and I thought that you two—and I never thought—oh, do don't be angry with me; I thought it would be so nice," and a fresh tap was turned on which threatened to wash the white waistcoat quite away.

"Dear me!" exclaimed Jones, "*That* never struck me before; of course, the will says—why perhaps *that* is what Tryson meant; if so—"

"Oh, I'm sure of it."

"Are you? Well; dear me, dear me, what a mess I have made of it. It certainly would be a better match in every respect for both parties; and I think —" but again Jones did not say what he thought, and only looked at the carpet,

"You're not angry!" said Tilly raising her head and looking slily at him.

"If the widow marries before Tilly," mused Jones abstractedly, "she forfeits half her fortune to me, so that if she marries me it is the same as no forfeiture. Ah, I see!"

"Yes," said Tilly, looking up archly at him; "and if mamma marries before I am twenty-one then I—"

"I see what you mean; then *you* can get married as soon as she does. Oh, Miss Sly-boots ought'nt you to be ashamed of yourself to plot against your old guardian this way."

"Don't scold; tell me you're not angry with me."

"No, no," replied he smiling, "now run away and leave me to see if I can't plot a little; but Tilly you needn't tell anyone, that is, it's not necessary for anybody to know what an old fool—"

"Don't you ever say another word about that again, and I never will, there," and she kissed him again and ran laughing out of the office.

Then Jones sat down and hatched his diabolical plot, and several times he laughed to himself as if it was quite a merry matter he was thinking of. At last he drew a sheet of paper towards him and commenced to write.

The letter was to the widow, and Jones told a lot of stories in it; for he said that he did not understand what she had written him about marrying Tilly; that he never had any such intention; that Tilly was engaged to Mr. Stedman; that she had confessed it to him and asked his help; that he had thought what an easy way out of the difficulty it would be if he could persuade her [Mrs. Tyson] to marry him [Jones]; and how in trying to tell her of his love and Tilly's engagement at the same time he got the two subjects mixed, and, probably created a wrong impression in her mind. He wound up with an offer of his hand and heart and an intimation that he would call in the evening for his answer.

It was an artfully written letter and put the widow a little at disadvantage as long as she did not know that he had actually proposed to Tilly; and so Jones thought after he had despatched the boy with it, and he laughed quietly at his own cleverness.

The widow did not prove obdurate, and Jones was made a happy man that evening. A double wedding took place the following February, the widow and Jones being the first couple united, so that by a legal fiction Tilly did not lose her fortune. The quartette spent the honeymoon in Europe, and then settled down at Alaska Villa where they now are with a couple of little Jones' and Stedman's making the house young again with their squalls.

Jones' boy is Jones' boy no longer. The four years which have elapsed since my story opened have transformed him into Jones' duly articled clerk, and he talks largely of what he will do when he is "called to the bar." He is quite a swell now, has all his clothes made by a fashionable tailor whom he "promises" to pay; smokes cheap cigars which generally make him sick; cultivates assiduously three or four red hairs under his nose which he pompously refers to as his "moustache," and boasts of taking his "girl" out driving and to the theatre. In short he sets up for a "fashionable" young man, and gives promise of coming to no good end unless he materially alters his mode of life.

Out of the Snow.

OUT OF THE SNOW.

It was Christmas Eve and a light snow was filling the air with fleecy particles, whirling and wheeling gracefully about and gradually covering the streets and housetops with its pure white robe. It was early in the evening, although the lamps had long been lighted, and the fitful gas disseminated its feeble rays on the thronged and busy street. Along St. James and Notre Dame streets, merry crowds thronged the way, and laughed and sang as they went on their way home laden with Christmas gifts, or burthened with loads of good things intended to grace the Christmas table on the morrow. The great crowd kept surging on, crowding the highways and branching off into St. Lambert, Bleury and other side streets. Gay sleighs spun with lightning-like rapidity over the frozen snow, and the merry tinkle of their cheerful bells broke out on the frosty air. The whole world seemed filled with gladness, and one seraphic shout of joy burst from the crushing crowd; all hurried along so intent on the universal joy or general plea-

sure that they failed to notice one sad form—one
crouching figure—one breaking heart, thrown down
in the utter exhaustion of its hopelessness, lying
prone on the frozen snow in front of the French
Church, with its weary head resting on the iron
rails.

It was a girlish figure, crouched up for warmth
and but thinly covered by the light summer dress
and scant shawl; her head was uncovered, and the
drifting snow was forming in little heaps on the
dark auburn curls which fell in heavy masses over
her shoulders. The face was wan, and pinched with
want and suffering, but its clear oval outline, fair complexion and general *contour* gave evidence of beauty
under more favorable circumstances. And there she
lay in a death-like sleep or torpor, with the wild
crowd swaying past her in their glee, and the snow
falling in masses about her and threatening to envelope her in its cold embrace, and usher her into the
spirit land through its frozen medium.

* * * * * *

Mr. Alfred Johnson stood before his desk in the warm
counting house in his employer's office in St. Paul
street, on that same Christmas Eve, and reviewed his
own private affairs for the past year. He was young,
probably not over two or three and twenty, fair
haired, with a fine open forehead, but rather an un-
certain expression in his clear blue eyes. He was
making up an account; and his brows grew con-

tracted and his manner more and more serious as the balance slowly but surely showed itself to be heavily on the wrong side. It was his own private account with his employer, which, as cashier, he could "bridge over" during the year, but which would now have to stand the severe test of the books being balanced by the bookkeeper—an old enemy—and the personal scrutiny of his employer, a most exact and careful man of business, who, although he had every confidence in Alfred, whom he had known from childhood, would, as a matter of business, make minute examination of the accounts at the close of the year, so as to see exactly how his affairs stood.

The account was finished, and, examine it how he would, Alfred found the balance over five hundred dollars against him; which was clearly money of his employer's which he had appropriated during the year. He was by no means what would be called a bad young man; he was a good son and brother, had worked up to his present responsible position by steady industry and strict integrity; his salary was a good one, and he contributed most of it to the support of his widowed mother and two sisters, younger than himself, who had been thrown almost entirely on him when his father died two years before.

Up to within the past year he had always been steady and wholly devoted to his mother and sisters; but during the last twelve months he had fallen into bad company, had got into the habit of spending the

evenings from home, and was seldom to be found in
the family circle after tea. He had got accustomed to
dropping into saloons for "a quiet drink and a
friendly game of cards;" and had also learned to play
billiards, a very expensive game to learn, as beginners
usually discover. His means soon proved inade-
quate to the new demands made on his purse, and
then—hard pressed for ready money—he was tempted
to "borrow" ten dollars from the thousands entrusted
to his care.

Of course he intended to return it; few men in
his circumstances ever commit a cool, deliberate robbery. The devil is very insidious with them, it is only
the "use'" of the money they want for a few days,
not the money itself, and it is so much easier to take
it temporarily from the funds committed to their
care than to borrow from a friend and stand the
chance of being refused, or having to explain why
the money is wanted. Youth is very hopeful, the
darkness of to-day is sure to be dispelled by the
imaginary brightness of to-morrow, and the present
difficulty is in fancy overcome by the success of the
future. "I shall be able to return it in a little while,"
is the bait with which the evil one catches most of
his youthful defaulters, and is the one hardest for
them to resist.

So it was with Alfred Johnson; he felt confident
of being able to return that first ten dollars; but the
day of return never came, and, the first false step

being taken, he kept sinking deeper and deeper into defalcation, driven madly onwards by the hope of being by some means able to make restitution, until now he stood involved beyond all hope of extrication.

He closed the book with a heavy sigh and sat down to think about it. Look at it any way he would, there seemed but one path out of the difficulty, to plunge deeper in, to take two or three thousand dollars more from the large sums of which he had full control and escape to the United States with his ill-gotten gains, and try, by leading a better and more steady life in that land of promise, to recover the sum he had misappropriated, and by an earnest, useful life, recover, if possible, his own self-esteem and the respect of all good men, which he would forfeit as soon as his crime was known.

But that way meant disgrace to the name he bore, and which had been handed down to him stainless by an honest and upright father; it meant shame to the grey hairs of his mother, and sorrow to his fond and loving sisters; it meant more than that, it meant destruction to all hope of another and a different love which had, almost without his knowing it, been growing up in his heart; he might prosper in the States, but he would be disgraced and friendless in Canada. And yet, to stay and be publicly tried as a defaulter? for that would be the alternative. He knew his employer to be a kind, but just and honest man who would not overlook his misconduct, lest it

should prove a bad example to others. The problem
was too hard to solve, and he sat with his head buried
in his hands, thinking bitterly over it.

At last he was resolved; the evil day of discovery
could not be put off for more than a week, as the books
would be balanced at the opening of the new year
and then discovery was inevitable: he, therefore,
determined to make his preparations at once, break
the sad intelligence as kindly as possible to his mother
and sister, and start for the States before the year ran
out. Settling the matter thus in his mind he wrapped
himself in his overcoat, and pulling his cap well
down over his ears went out into the night.

His way was up St. Sulpice street, and as he bent
forward against the keen air at the corner of Notre
Dame St., he stumbled against a crouching figure
and almost fell. Stooping to see who it was lying
exposed to the storm, Alfred noticed that it was a girl;
the face was pale and wan, and frost marks were coming out on the cheek and nose. The girl raised her head
for a moment when he struck against her, but quickly
returned to her recumbent position and seemed to be
thoroughly numbed by the cold, and fast freezing to
death. Alfred was kind-hearted almost to a fault,
and the sight of this lone suffering girl moved him
greatly; he shook her gently by the shoulder and
tried to move her.

"Get up, get up, my girl; if you lie here much
longer you will freeze to death." The girl stirred a

little when he spoke to her; and as he continued shaking her, with his assistance, rose to her feet.

"Why don't you go home?"

She gazed dreamily about for a minute, then said slowly and sadly,

"I have no home."

"Where is your father?"

"I don't know. I don't know if I have one now."

"Where is your mother; why don't you go to her?"

"I am going to her, I hope; she is in Heaven."

"Have you no friends."

"None."

Alfred was puzzled and scarcely knew what to do. The girl stood half leaning against the iron rail, and half supported by him; but her momentary strength seemed fast giving way, and he could feel her weight growing heavier on his arm. What should he do with her? Should he take her to the Police Station, or to the Hospital, or some charitable institution? The idea of abandoning her in the snow never occurred to him for a moment. His difficulty was solved for him by a passing carter calling out gaily,

"Sleigh, sir?"

"Yes," he said, as an idea occurred to him. "Take me to No. — Dorchester street." He thought as he half lifted the girl into the sleigh and tenderly supported her, "I'll take her to mother, she'll know what to do with her, and to-morrow or next day we will see what can be done for her. It would be rather too hard to let a girl freeze to death on Christmas Eve."

Mrs. Johnson was very much surprised at the strange companion her son brought home with him; but she was a kind hearted woman, although weak and foolish, and the poor girl was well tended and gently and tenderly nursed.

But want and exposure had too surely done their work, and brain fever quickly set in. The doctor, whom Alfred called to attend her, gave no hope of her recovery; nature was too much exhausted, he said, and although she may rally a little and regain her reason, the system was too much shaken for her to regain her health, and she would probably sink from debility. The girl remained unconscious all night and the next day, not raving, but moaning and muttering incoherently; and Mrs. Johnson and her daughter, nursed her tenderly and carefully.

* * * * * * * *

Christmas Day did not pass off very joyfully at the Johnsons'. Alfred was "out of sorts," as his mother expressed it, and rather disposed to be pettish, so that the dinner was rather a stiff affair, and there was little conversation after. It was late in the evening when Alfred, returning from a walk, found his mother seated by the bed-side of the still unconscious girl. He had made up his mind that the disclosure of his crime must be made to his mother now, and he was very pale and ill at ease as he took a seat by her, fully determined to tell her all. As he seated himself he glanced toward the bed and asked how the girl was.

"A little quieter," replied his mother, "she has just fallen into a light sleep."

"Mother, I want to tell you something; something that will make you ashamed of me, perhaps, but you must know it sometime, and it is best you heard it from me." He drew a stool to her feet and hiding his face in her lap, told her all.

Mrs. Johnson was a weak-minded woman who was more accustomed to take advice from her son than to give it; and she was totally unfitted to offer him any good counsel, or to persuade him from his mad desire to run away. She saw only the danger of his remaining, and already pictured to herself her darling placed in the felon's dock, and condemned to the prison cell. All her love and fear was roused for her son, and she not only approved of his intention of going to the States, but besought him through her tears to go at once and not risk the chance of discovery by remaining in Montreal.

"Go, go at once, Alfred," she said, "you have done wrong, but you are young and can and will repent and pay back all you have taken. Don't run the risk of Mr. Homespun's discovering you, for I know he is a hard man, although a just one, and he will have no mercy."

"Do not go," said a sweet clear voice, and mother

and son both turned instinctively toward the bed
from whence the sound proceeded, and saw the girl
they had thought asleep sitting up, with the light of
reason once more in her eyes, but an excited, wild
look in her face. " Don't go, don't go," she cried,
speaking rapidly and with increasing excitement ;
"I have heard all; forgive me for listening ; I did
not mean to, but I could not help it. I know you
have been good and kind to me; I remember your
taking me out of the snow, and I know gentle hands
have been nursing me. It comes like a dream, I
cannot put it all together ; but I am sure you have a
good heart, and did not intend to do wrong. Go to
your employer, tell him what you have done and ask
him to forgive you, and give you a chance to regain
his confidence. If he is a good and Christian man
he will be merciful with a sinner as he hopes for
mercy hereafter from the great and merciful God who
says, ' Judge not that ye be not judged.' Oh, do not
do this thing; don't bring shame on the name you
bear, sorrow and disgrace on those who love you. I
have seen it; I have seen a wife's heart broken and a
daughter almost reduced to shame, when all might
have been well, with a little courage to speak the
truth, and a little faith in God to judge the intent and
not the deed. Go to your employer, tell him all,
throw yourself on his mercy, and ask him to forgive
you ; do not increase the wrong you have already
done by further injuring or deceiving him. Confess

to him now; he will pardon you. I know he will;
I can see it. Tell him the poor girl—you—saved
———."

Her voice had grown strong with the excitement
which was working in her, her face had flushed as she
bent her body forward, her earnest, pleading tones,
her fervent impressive manner seemed like one inspired, and her two auditors sat spell bound as if listening to the words of prophecy. She broke off abruptly,
her face blanched, her gaze became fixed and rigid, a
faint sigh broke from her lips, quickly followed by a
small stream of blood, she fell heavily back upon her
pillow, and before mother or son could reach the bed-
side, the soul of the poor outcast had winged its way
to its Maker.

* * * * * * *

Three days passed; the poor friendless girl was
placed in the strangers' vault, for no one knew her
name nor where she came. On an old worn pocket
handkerchief was found marked the word "Marian,"
and by that name she was entered on the funeral
register. Alfred alone accompanied the body to the
cemetery, and as he stood beside the plain, unorna-
mented coffin a strange superstitious feeling came over
him, and he thought he could hear that sweet earnest
voice saying, "Go to your employer, tell him what
you have done, ask him to forgive you and give you
another chance."

He could not shake off the feeling, and that night

in his dreams he again saw the animated and inspired face, and again the words rang in his ear, "Confess to him now; he will pardon; I know he will."

Next morning he went to the office with a firm determination of telling Mr. Homespun everything, but somehow he put it off and it was not till after dinner that he found courage to enter Mr. Homespun's private office, and ask him for an interview. Even then he almost lost courage, and it was only with the greatest difficulty that he managed at last to get out in broken, disjointed sentences a confession of his guilt. He did not spare himself, but told what his intention had been, how he had meant to take more and go to the States, but he did not tell what had caused him to change his determination.

Mr. Homespun sat and listened in wonder, almost doubting the evidence of his senses. He had known Alfred from childhood, and regarded him almost as a son; but there was a good deal of the Spartan about him, and he thought it was his duty to society to expose the crime and ingratitude of the boy whom he loved better than anything on earth except his daughter Fannie.

"Alfred," he said—and the old man's voice was pained and broken so that Alfred scarcely recognised it—"what you have told me has given me greater pain than anything I have heard since it pleased the Almighty to take my own son from me. Had anyone else told me, I should not have believed it, but your

confession leaves no room for doubt. I have loved
you Alfred, and I hoped some day to reward your
services with an interest in my business; but now I
must do my duty."

The old man paused for a moment, and before he spoke
again, the door leading into the outer office was thrown
open, and a bright, sunny-haired girl of about eighteen
or nineteen came running in, and pulling a chair close
up to the cheery wood-fire burning in the grate, put
her feet on the fender, and, giving a little lady-like
shiver, commenced poking the fire vigorously, declaring she was freezing to death.

"Come, you old papa," she said, looking over at Mr.
Homespun," "no more business to day; I have come
to capture you and take you off sleigh-riding; no excuse," she continued—going over to his chair and
throwing her arms round his neck—"or I'll pull all
your dear old whiskers out."

As she stood behind her father's chair she shot one
rapid meaning glance at Alfred, but he stood with his
head bent down gazing intently on the carpet, and
the hot blood rising rapidly in his face; it was hard,
very hard, he thought that Fannie should be the first
to hear of his disgrace.

The girl saw at a glance that there was something
wrong, and looking from one face to the other she
left her father's side, and crossing to Alfred laid her
hand on his shoulder and said, half playfully, "What
is the matter, has Alfred been a naughty boy and

that cross papa of mine been scolding him? Well it serves him right, for he greatly needs to improve his manners. I think, sir, you might have spoken to me when I came in; and your conduct lately has been shameful, you haven't been to see me for over a week. Don't make any excuses about business, for I shant believe them; and don't ever speak to me again."

Her tone was half bantering, half earnest, but the look which accompanied them was full of meaning, and as Mr. Homespun looked up and saw it, it let in a flood of light on his mind, and he began to wonder at his own blindness. Alfred and Fannie had grown up together as brother and sister, and it had never occurred to the old man, totally absorbed in his one child, that the brotherly and sisterly feeling might grow into a deeper and stronger affection. Now he saw in an instant that, on one side at least, it had; and his duty did not seem quite so clear to him.

"Fannie," he said very gravely, "I cannot go with you to-day; Alfred and I have a very serious matter to talk over, and I cannot leave the office."

"Well, bring Alfred with you and you can scold him all you want to; I shan't ask you to spare him."

At last she had her own way, and her father consented to go, but nothing further was said about Alfred's accompanying them. As they were leaving the room Mr. Homespun said with great emphasis to Alfred, who had remained motionless during the short dialogue.

"I shall expect to meet you *here* on my return; do not leave the country without seeing me again."

"Leave the country!" exclaimed Fanny, turning pale for a moment, then flushing up again, "where is he going?"

"I think," said Mr. Homespun, speaking very slowly and evidently with difficulty, "that the prospect Alfred has of advancement in the United States is too good for me, as a friend, to advise him to refuse it. His absence will probably be a long one, possibly he may remain there altogether."

He laid great stress on the last few words, and Alfred felt that he was pardoned, but with the condition that he left Canada.

Fannie said nothing more, but walked out of the office, evidently wanting to be alone for a few minutes if possible, for she looked very much as if she wished to indulge in that great female luxury, a good cry.

When she had left the office, Mr. Homespun turned to Alfred and said, "You shall go to the States; I have a friend in New York who will take you into his office, and you will have another chance. Be careful that you make good use of it. You will leave to-morrow, but you must never return to Canada."

He went towards the door, and as he was passing through, shook his head sadly and said to himself, "I am not at all clear that I have done my duty, but—."

He did not finish the sentence, but followed Fannie to the sleigh.

* * * * * * * *

Alfred went to the States, and entered on his new duties. His lesson had been a sharp and severe one, but he profited by it. He had no idea of remaining in the States all his life, and by steady industry and good conduct, in two years he so raised himself in his employer's estimation, that he was promoted to a very responsible position, and sent to Canada on special business by the firm.

It is very easy to see how it ended. Fannie had not changed during the two years, and Alfred had found out by absence how dear to him Fannie was. And Mr. Homespun? Well he did not like it much at first; but he went to New York and satisfied himself that Alfred's conduct during his two years' exile had been perfectly exemplary, and when Fannie teased him for his consent to their union he could not resist long, and seemed to have no difficulty at all in seeing clearly that he had "done his duty."

Oh dear! its twenty years ago now since that Christmas Eve which proved so eventful in the career of Alfred Johnson, and Mr. Homespun has long since been gathered to his fathers, and Alfred has succeeded to the business and is now one of our leading and most prosperous and most honored merchants, and talks of retiring and "taking it easy."

Mr. Homespun kept his secret well, and no one—

not even Fannie—ever knew how near the brink of ruin he had stood. Fannie is a sober little matron now, and many young olive branches adorn the family tree. But whenever Christmas Eve comes around there always returns to Alfred the memory of that Christmas Eve, twenty years ago, when he had stood on the verge of disgrace, and then comes to him the vision of a plain marble cross with the word "Marian" on it, and he thinks of the unknown, friendless girl whose good advice saved him, and who came to him " Out of the Snow."

Christmas in the Flies.

CHRISTMAS IN THE FLIES.

A CURTAIN MAN'S STORY.

CHAPTER I.

ON DUTY.

PERHAPS you don't know what a curtain man is, and very likely you never heard of any other flies than those that buzz about in the summer time, or those you drive about in in rainy weather; but I don't mean those sort of flies, I mean the flies of a theatre; the place up over the stage which the audience never sees, and which they know nothing about; and I'm the man that tends up in the flies and pulls the curtain up and lets it down.

It's a queer place to be for three hours or so while the play is going on forty or fifty feet below, and queer sights we see sometimes looking down; things not meant to be seen, and not set down on the bills. I've watched many a curious performance, and witnessed more than one serious accident during the years I've been at work in the flies; but one of the saddest I ever saw occurred a few years ago when I was at work in an East End theatre in London, and it took place on a Christmas Day.

There wasn't any performance that night, but there was a full rehearsal called for the pantomime, which was to be brought out on Boxing-night; and I was giving the scene-shifters a hand, managing the borders and such things, up in the flies.

I may as well explain that the borders are those strips of muslin painted to imitate woods, or clouds, or ceilings, as the case may be, which hang across the stage, and have to be changed when the scene and wings change; and, also that a platform gallery runs down each side over the wings, so that the scene shifters can move about from place to place as necessity may require.

It was a heavy scenic pantomime, and what with transformations, and quick changes, and new effects to try, and new machinery to get into good working order, we had a busy time of it.

There was one scene, the last transformation, which was expected to be very fine, and on which the success of the piece to a great extent depended; it was called "The Fairies Grotto of Delight," or some such thing, and amongst other effects a number of fairies were to be suspended in mid air, and lowered by a windlass to within a few feet of the head of the Fairy Queen, who was to stand in a vast flower in the centre of the stage. This was rather a difficult thing to do; and the ballet girls who personated the fairies were a little nervous at first, and half afraid to trust themselves to the ropes which were to suspend them.

I was rather late in getting to the theatre, for I lived some distance away, and I hurried up into the flies at once as rehearsal had commenced.

Just as I reached my place I met Jim Harkins, one of the stage carpenters who worked in the flies.

"A Merry Christmas to you, Jim," I said.

"Me ? Christmas be hanged," he answered quite gruffly and shortly for him, for Jim was a civil-spoken, quiet young fellow, who was well liked in the flies and a regular favorite with all who knew him. I took another look at him as he spoke, and noticed there was something wrong, he seemed out of sorts and wasn't paying attention to his business, which was unusual with him, but looking down at the stage most of the time.

"What's wrong, Jim?"

"Nothing; haul that front border up a little, it fouls the flat."

He turned away, and I didn't say any more at the time, but I watched him, and from his looking down at the stage so much I got looking at it myself, but I soon began to watch the actors and actresses off the stage rather than those on it.

It's curious work to sit up away over everybody's head and watch what is going on without being seen and I soon got quite interested. There were a good many people about the theatre that night besides the regular company, although there was no performance, for it was a full dress rehearsal and the manager had invited a number of the critics of the different newspapers and some friends of his own to have a private view of the new piece. Most of them were in front, but some of the favored ones were behind the scenes, either in the green-room or at the wings, talking and laughing with the actors and actresses and the ballet girls, and somehow I fell to watching the wings more than any other place, and many nice quiet little flirtations I saw that were never intended for my view.

I know most of the company and was pretty well acquainted with the ballet, for my wife had been a ballet girl in this same theatre, and we often had some of them up to tea with us on a Sunday night; and I amused myself during the time I could spare from duty watching some of them "cutting up." It was fun to me to see some of them quietly poking fun at the "nobs" who had got behind the scenes, for perhaps the first time, and many a quiet little laugh I had all to myself.

I noticed one young swell in particular who didn't appear ever to have been behind the scenes before and who seemed to be looking for something, as he kept peeping about this way and that, getting tangled up in the flats sometimes, and occasionally losing himself amongst the scenery to the great amusement of

the girls, and to the great annoyance of the stage
carpenters who swore at him, but in low tones, for he
appeared to be a great friend of the manager's, and it
would not do to insult a friend of his.

He was quite a handsome young gentleman, tall
and well formed, and with a slightly aristocratic air
about him which well became his classic cast of features.
He strolled about half listlessly, now exchanging
a few words with some acquaintance, and occasionally
speaking for a minute to the manager; but I
noticed that he kept glancing about him, not with an
air of vulgar curiosity, but like a man in search of
something.

I got quite interested in this young gentleman, and
watched him in an idly curious way while I waited
for the end of the scene to change for the ballet which
was to come next.

Just before the signal was given to change I saw
him lift his hat to some one, who was out of sight
from where I stood, and advance with a pleased smile
of recognition on his face. The next instant the
prompter's whistle sounded and I was busy changing
the scene for the ballet, and when I got through he
was leaning against a wing alone, watching the girls
practice a new dance.

I never did understand much about these ballet
divertisements, as they are called; which pretend to
express all sorts of passions and emotions by a series
of jumps, pirouettes, posturings, and facial and bodily

contortions, often of the ugliest and least graceful kinds. Ballet pantomime was always too difficult a conundrum for me to solve; when I have seen a *coryphee* dancing around one of the characters in the ballet, now taking long, sliding steps, then short, quick jumps in the air, kicking her feet quickly together two or three times the while; then making various spirited and vigorous kicks at the nose of the person she was dancing around; next revolving rapidly on one toe until she assumed somewhat the appearance of an insane teetotum of peculiar shape; and finally throwing herself on one knee with one leg very much extended the body bent backwards until her head almost touched the ground, and her arms held up to the central figure—which has stood stock-still and exhibited no more emotion than a pump; I could not, for the life of me, fancy that it was intended to show her love and devotion to the object of her affection until I was told so. I have seen a little dog go through a somewhat similar performance at sight of his master, the principal differences being that the little dog barked with joy and the *coryphee* didn't; and that the *coryphee* exposed her person rather unnecessarily and indecently, and the little dog didn't. I confess, I am r̲   ̲ partial to ballets, and I don't think many ̲ ̲ ̲ really admire them for what they call the "p̲ ̲ ̲ motion," and the "grace of action," and all that rubbish; just put the ballet girls into pantaloons and high-necked dresses, and very few people would find any grace or poetry in it.

I never derived much pleasure from sitting up in the flies watching the ballet, but this night I was particularly interested; for Betty Langley, the only daughter of my old friend Dick Langley, who used to play Harlequin in the pantomime for many years at our theatre, and who had died about two years ago, was to make her first appearance as a solo dancer the following night; and I was anxious to see how she acquitted herself in the hopping and skipping and pirouetting line.

Betty was about eighteen, small, beautifully formed and "pretty as a picture," as the saying is. She had been in the ballet a little more than a year, and by close attention to her business had made herself a favorite with the manager, who had promoted her to a leading part in the new ballet. You must not suppose, however, that she was announced on the bills as Betty Langley; Oh, no! that would have been altogether too common and plebian, so the bills informed the public that "Signora Bettini Langleggi" would make her "first appearance" in the new pantomime.

It must be confessed that the name was not a pretty one, and implied a great injustice to Betty's pedal extremities which were short and elegantly shaped; but it sounded foreign, at least the manager thought so, and that was a great point; for it is a well-known and generally accepted fact in theatrical circles that although an English, Irish or American girl may have as fine a voice as Grissi, or be more graceful than Taglioni, yet it is almost impossible for her to get credit for being able to sing or dance, if she appears under an English name. It stands to reason; how would it look on the bills to announce "Miss Mary Smith, the celebrated singer;" or "Miss Jane Brown, the eminent dancer?" Only Frenchify it a bit and see how much grander it looks to put on the bills "Mademoiselle Marietta Smitherrinni, the world renowned cantatrice," (whom nobody ever heard of before) or "Signora Juanita Brownoroso, *premier danseuse* to H. I. H. the Emperor of Nooneknowswhere." It is all very fine for Shakespeare to ask "What's in a name?" I tell you there is a good deal in a name, especially in the theatrical profession. And so the manager of our theatre changed Betty's name for her to Langleggi, and the first thing she knew of it was seeing it announced in the bills.

Betty got through her dance in splendid style; and even the manager applauded when she finished, and paid her some very high compliments. She did not wait long to hear them, for the stage was cold and her dress light, but hurried away towards the wing where the swell I had already noticed was standing, with a long cloak over his arm, which he threw around her as she approached, and said something which appeared to please or amuse her; for she drew back with a merry laugh and a low, half-mocking bow, which I had often seen her make when she was in high spirits.

He bent over her a little as they moved off side by side towards the green room, for she did not come on again until the last scene but one, and I thought he stooped down to her rather closer than was necessary. I could not get a very good view from where I stood, and I might have been mistaken, but I thought she blushed as she turned away, and glanced up into the flies for an instant, as if looking for some one.

CHAPTER II.

ON THE WATCH.

I WAS rather astonished and grieved at what I had seen, for Betty was almost like a daughter to me, and I took more than a common interest in her, not only for her own sake but for that of her father, who had been a bosom friend of mine for years; and I didn't like the idea of this young swell walking away with her in that familiar manner. I knew Betty was as pure and good a girl as ever lived, altho' she did dance for a living, and I did not fear her coming to harm; I knew her too well for that; but I was afraid that this young swell might fill her head with foolish notions of grandeur which might keep her heart away from a good honest man who wanted to make her his wife; and I was on the point of leaving the flies with the intention of speaking to her when I was seized by the arm with a pretty tight grip, and a voice said almost in my ear:

"Jobson, did you see that?"

I turned to the speaker and saw Jim Harkins standing by my side. His face was deathly pale, his teeth clenched tightly together, his eyes blazing, and he squeezed my arm so hard it almost made me cry out.

"See what?" I answered, more to gain time than for any other reason.

"That fellow making love to Betty," he answered, grinding his teeth in a way that seemed to turn all the blood in me to sour milk and send a frozen ramrod down my back.

"Making love?" I said in a tone of surprise. "I saw him speak to her; that was all."

"That wasn't all; he was making love to her, and she liked it."

"Come, come, now Jim," I said, trying to get him a bit cool, "you ought to be ashamed of yourself to speak of Betty like that. There isn't a truer hearted girl in the world than she is, and when she gave her word be sure her heart went with it, and won't change; so don't be a jealous fool."

"Jealous!" he replied with a sneer and a couple of grinds at his teeth that ought to have dislocated his jaw-bone. "Jealous! That's always the way. The moment a man shows any anxiety at the conduct of the girl he loves it's 'He's jealous.' That's what Betty said this morning when I spoke to her about it."

"Oh, ho!" I said, "you've been talking to her about it, have you; and you've had a lover's quarrel, I suppose."

"We've had no quarrel. I told her it wasn't proper to have that fellow dangling after her; that was all."

"How can he have been 'dangling after her;' I never saw him before to-night, and I don't think Betty ever did."

"You don't know everything, Jobson, altho' you think you do. He has been meeting her nearly every Sunday for over a month, and paying her a good deal of attention, and I won't stand it any longer. We must come to an understanding to-night; if she wants to have that swell make love to her, well and good; but she is no wife for Jim Harkins," and he ground his teeth again so terribly that I felt all over ice and needles.

"Look here, Jim," I said, "do stop grinding your teeth that way; or, if you must grind them, put your finger, or a piece of rubber, or something in your mouth so that you can feel the satisfaction of grinding away without making that disagreeable noise which sets my teeth on edge, and makes me feel like pins and needles all over. And what nonsense are you talking about Betty meeting this swell every Sunday for a month? Why she and her mother have taken tea with my wife and I nearly every Sunday evening since Dick died; and I am sure that swell chap never was in my house."

"Who said he was? Don't Betty go to other places besides your house? Don't she go to see the manager's wife almost every Sunday afternoon; and

don't that fellow drop in there 'by chance' whenever
she is there ? Don't tell me; I know all about it only
too well, and I tell you this thing's got to be put a
stop to; and to night too."

I could'nt say a word for a minute or two, I was so
astonished. If some one had told me that Mrs. Jobson had eloped with all our eleven children I could
not have been more surprised, and I could only sit
and stare at Jim without saying a word. I know
there must be some mistake or misunderstanding somewhere ; but where ? I would have staked my life on
Betty's truth and innocence, but why had she never
said anything about having met this man at the manager's ? It wasn't Betty's nature to be secret or sly
about anything; when Jim Harkins asked her, at the
wing, while she was waiting to go on one night, if she
would marry him, she told me of it while we were
walking home together after the performance ; and
there never was any new acquaintance she formed, or
any little trouble she had but what my wife and I
know of it; then why had she never mentioned to us
her meeting this man ?

I know she loved Jim, and they were to be married
as soon as Betty got her salary raised—for Jim could
not afford to take her off the stage at once, and Betty's
mother being an invalid was totally dependent on her
for support—but why should she take to flirting with
swells just at this time, when she would never speak
to one of them before she was engaged, and had the

reputation of being the strictest girl in her conduct in the whole theatre? I confess it puzzled me, and I could not make it out. All at once an idea came into my head, and I said:

"Jim, I have an idea that ——"

"Phe-e-e-e-e-e-w!" went the prompter's whistle to change the scene, and Jim and I had to go different parts of the flies, and I didn't have a chance to tell him what I had thought.

This was the scene immediately before the ballet, and we were kept pretty busy getting ready for the grand transformation scene, fixing the windlass, arranging the fly borders, etc., and the machinist was preparing his magnesium lights to throw on from above. Jim was working in the gallery over me adjusting the ropes which were to suspend the fairies in the last scene and I could not speak to him.

The scene was more than half over when the ballet began to gather at the wings, ready for their scene; and a few seconds after I saw Betty come out of the green room and stand at the wing in fourth groove, from which place she was to make her entrance.

She was to dance a Spanish dance in this scene, at least I think it was a Spanish dance but could not be very sure; I know a long, light gauze scarf had something to do with it, and Betty had this scarf wound round her head and neck as she stood waiting, and it struck me at the moment that I had never seen her look half so handsome as she did standing there in her flimsy ballet skirt with that light diaphanous mass of white scarf floating about her.

She did not stand there long alone, for the swell, whom I had not seen since he went away with her, suddenly appeared again, and taking his place by her side, entered at once into conversation with her.

I watched them close now, and noticed that altho' Betty appeared pleased at his attention, she did not seem quite at her ease, but kept glancing up into the flies in an anxious manner as if afraid that Jim or I was watching her.

I was, that was sure; but she could not see me as I was hidden behind the borders; whether Jim was or not I could not tell, but I saw him out on a little staging at the extreme back helping the machinist arrange his lights, and I did not think he could see her from where he was.

CHAPTER III.

ON FIRE.

The scene soon changed, and Betty did her solo. Again she was successful, and again she received the plaudits of the manager and his friends. She was all flushed and triumphant as she went back to her place at the wing while the ballet finished, and I saw her smile proudly as the swell spoke to her.

He did not say much; but I saw him put his hand in his pocket, take out a paper and hand it to her with a smile, and then she gave a little cry of delight, clasped her hands for a moment, and then suddenly seizing his hand she pressed it to her lips.

At that instant there was a sudden dazzling stream of light thrown from above; the lime light had been turned on the pair with startling-suddenness and Betty jumped away in affright at the unexpected shock.

How can I describe what followed.

The scene was all set for the transformation; there were gas jets in all parts of the stage, and Betty in her terror sprang so near one of them that the light gauze scarf blew against it, and quicker than tongue can tell or pen can write her head and neck were wrapped in flame, and the poor, half-maddened girl was rushing towards the foot-lights.

A scream of horror and terror broke from all present; the poor ballet girls rushed about in all directions endeavoring to save their own light clothing from contact with the fiery element, and the utmost confusion reigned ; but high above all other sounds came a fearful cry from the very top of the theatre,

"My God, I have killed her!"

I involuntarily looked up for an instant and there stood Jim Harkins on the little platform, sixty feet above the stage, looking like one beside himself. Some of the ropes by which the ballet girls were to be suspended hung near him, and before I could even think he had seized one of the longest, sprung from the platform, and was sliding rapidly down to the stage. It was a terrible feat for anyone but a practiced acrobat, as the rope was at least twenty feet too short, but love or madness supplied the place of skill, and almost as quick as thought he slid to the end of the rope, fell lightly and safely to the stage, and darted toward the blazing figure.

But he was a moment too late. The swell had been almost as quick as Jim, only he had paused an instant to seize the heavy shawl which Betty had left at the wing when she went on to dance ; and just as Jim reached the stage the shawl was flung around the burning girl, and she was thrown to the floor, while the swell bent over her and endeavored to stifle the terrible fire.

"Stand back," cried Jim, thrusting the swell aside and kneeling beside the now motionless figure of the poor girl. "Oh, my darling! my darling! I've murdered you!" and the great, strong man threw himself down on the stage and sobbed in his agony.

We had got up some tidy sensations at our theatre during my time, and we had had some of the most celebrated actors and actresses play there; but never had there been anything before so terribly real and yet so dramatic as the scene that night.

There lay poor Betty motionless almost in the middle of the stage, with the shawl wrapped closely around her, and little spirals of smoke from the burnt dress and charred flesh still curling about her. She was a fearful sight; her face, neck, and arms were skinned, blackened with smoke, and fast swelling up; all that was left of her beautiful hair was a smoking mass of stumpy little black cinders clinging to her head, and her dress and underclothes were burnt into great holes, down to the skin. She was quite insensible, but an occasional spasmodic gasp, and a slight quivering of the limbs, showed that she was alive and sensible of pain. By her side, crouched down on his knees, his head buried in his hands, and his whole frame shaking with convulsive sobs, was Jim, with his coat off and his shirt sleeves rolled up, just as he had been at work; and at the back and wings stood the terrified ballet girls, supernumeraries, and others looking on in horror and dismay at the terrible tragedy which had been so suddenly enacted before them. It was the most awful, and at the same time the most dramatic "situation" I had ever seen, and I could not help thinking so as I hurried down out of the flies.

It had all passed like a flash; and I involuntarily looked at the wing where I had seen Betty only a moment before, and could scarcely realise that the charred, blackened, smoking, disfigured remnant of humanity before me, was the same happy, joyous, brilliant creature I had seen scarce thirty seconds ago in all the pride of her youth and beauty.

It was a wonderfully short scene to act, altho' a long one to describe; and it was all over before I could get to where Betty was lying.

The first person to regain his presence of mind—indeed, he seemed to be the only one who had never lost it—was the swell. He trembled violently, and seemed greatly agitated, but was as calm and collected as if the burning to death of ballet girls was an every-day affair with him, and not worth getting excited about; but it wasn't that; it was his immense self-control and power of keeping cool under trying circumstances, and I admired him for it.

"Here, my good man," he said, laying his hand on Jim's arm, "take her up and bring her into the green room, lift her carefully, she is terribly burned. Run for the nearest doctor," he continued to one of the stage hands standing by, "give him that card and tell him not to lose an instant; and, here, buy a pound of unslacked lime and a bottle of linseed oil from the chemist's on your way back." He put a card and a sovereign in the man's hand, having first written on the back of the card "Chalk," "Linseed Oil," so as to remind him what he was to bring in case he should forget the names, which was very possible in his excited state.

It is surprising how quickly one calm, cool, collected man can restore quiet and order in an excited crowd: no sooner had the swell issued his orders than everybody seemed to regain confidence and presence of mind. Jim lifted Betty tenderly and reverently in his arms, carried her to the green room and laid her on a sofa, which some gentle hands had already covered with shawls and other soft things for her to lie on.

A doctor was by her side by the time she was laid on the sofa, for there happened to be one present only he had been too much scared to say anything before. Restoratives were applied, and another man sent for a cooling lotion which the doctor ordered to bathe the wounds with, and after a little while Betty returned to something like consciousness; but she was in dreadful agony, groaned and moaned without ceasing, and could not articulate a word. The doctor said she had swallowed some of the fire and was scorched internally so that her recovery was very doubtful; only he did not say so in as plain terms, but used some long jaw-breaking Latin words which neither he nor any body else understood; but we all understood that poor Betty was in great danger, and altho' the manager dismissed the rehearsal at once, not one of the company left the theatre, but all waited anxiously to hear what the second doctor, who had just arrived, said.

I had left the green room and was going back to the flies to get my coat, for I had to break the terrible news to Betty's mother, when I saw something lying on the stage near the wing where Betty had been standing; it was the note the swell had given her just before Jim had thrown that fatal light on her; mechanically I picked it up and opened it, this was what it contained:

West End Theatre,
Christmas Day.

Dear Harcourt,

Mdlle. Jumpellini leaves me after the New Year, and I shall be in want of a Columbine; if your young *pro'ège* is only half as pretty and clever as you say—and I place great confidence in your judgment—she is just the girl for me; and if you are satisfied with her performance to-night, I authorize you to offer her £10 a week for three months, and possibly longer. She must be ready to open with me on 6th January. Wishing you the compliments of the season,

Believe me,
Ever yours truly,
O. BAGGS.

I carried the letter up into the flies with me and never took my eyes off it while I put my coat and hat on. I understood all about that swell now, just as well as if Betty had explained every word to me herself. I could tell what made her so civil and polite to him, and I knew why she kissed his hand out of gratitude. Yes, the whole thing came to me just as clearly as if it had been written out on a piece of paper; this man had met her at the manager's, and promissed to get her an engagement at a West End theatre, where she would get a salary large enough to enable her to marry; and she had kept it from us so that we might not be disappointed if she failed to get it; and have an agreeable surprise if she did. Poor girl, that innocent desire to surprise us all cost her her life.

When I returned to the green room, I saw by the faces of those at the door that there was no hope. The second doctor had just given his opinion; he said that she might live a few hours, but her internal injuries were too severe for her to recover; and it was very doubtful whether she would regain her consciousness or reason before she died.

Poor Jim stood by the sofa looking down at her he so loved, and had expected to make his wife, without uttering a word or moving a muscle; what he thought no man can tell, but his face showed the deep anguish he felt at the result of his jealous fit.

I broke the news to Mrs. Langley, who was ill in bed;

and leaving my wife with her returned to the theatre, the doctors having said that Betty must remain there as moving would kill her. I found everything pretty much the same as when I left: Betty was still moaning a little but had not spoken, and Jim stood still looking at her as if trying to impress her features on his mind so that they never could be erased; one of the doctors had gone, and nearly all the company, finding they could do nothing, had left the theatre; Mr. Harcourt was not in the green room, but I knew he was in the manager's room with him waiting for the end.

He had not long to wait.

A little before midnight she grew more restless, and seemed to be struggling to speak; the doctor touched Jim on the shoulder and said,

"Whisper to her."

He obeyed like one in a dream, and putting his lips close to her ear said,

"Betty, do you know me?"

She turned her head to him and put out her hand; she could not see, for her eyes were almost burnt out, and were bandaged down. Jim took the little, scorched hand in his and pressed it to his lips; something like a smile passed across her face, and with a great effort she articulated, very faintly, but distinctly, one word,

"Darling!"

And with that one word her spirit took its flight.

There isn't much left to tell. I found out afterwards that Mr. Harcourt was a clerk in the War Office, and also a very able critic, and had great influence with the managers, all of whom liked to have him visit them at their houses—as he always refused to go behind the scenes. He had met Betty two or three times at our manager's house, and taken quite a fancy to her. She had told him of her engagement and her hopes, and he had promised her that if she made a success in the new pantomime he would try to get her an engagement in a West End theatre where she could earn enough to enable her to marry and still support her mother comfortably. He had succeeded sooner and easier than he had expected, on account of Mdlle. Jumpellini breaking her contract with Mr. Baggs, and had come to the theatre to tell Betty her good fortune; the rest we know.

Jim Harkins never went back to the flies. He was soon told the whole story, and it seemed to break his heart to think he should have doubted Betty, and have caused her death. He loafed about London for a few weeks and then went to sea, and was lost in a storm some three years after in the Indian Ocean.

That was years ago, and I am rather too stiff in the back and weak in the knees now to tend the curtain, and I expect I shall soon have to give it up; but never a Christmas comes around but I think of my sweet little Betty and that memorable Christmas I spent in the flies.

Poetry.

A CHRISTMAS PRAYER.

Blessed Saviour, to whose praise
Dedicate we all this day,
Teach me how my thoughts to raise
Mould my lips the form to pray;
Guide me to that blest abode,
The Heaven of which Thou art a part,
Instil in me its holy love,
Make it Christmas in my heart.

As the sages did of yore
By thy manger bend the knee,
Asking simply to adore,
To behold and worship Thee;
So let me in spirit call
A vision of Thee as Thou art,
Saviour, Friend, Redeemer, All,
Make it Christmas in my heart.

Make me feel that Thou wilt hear
My humble sueing at thy feet;
Make me conscious Thou art near
Whatever danger I may meet;
Oh give me strength to cling to Thee
So that we never more may part,
Then shall I know 'twill truly be
Eternal Christmas in my heart.

DREAMLAND.

Oh, call me not back to my earthly abode,
From roaming through dreamland with those that I
love;
Oh, break not the spell by which shadowy thread
I was linked with the loved ones, the absent and
dead.

I dreamt of my boyhood, so joyous and free
Ere the cares of the world had grown heavy on me,
Forgot was my sorrow, unheeded my pain,
In the bright, sunny days of my boyhood again.

I dreamt of my mother, so gentle and kind,
My sister, whose light laugh threw care to the wind;
My father's fond smile, and my brother's loud
cheer,
Now where are the loved ones? Sad echo sighs,
"Where?"

From the home of my childhood I've faded away,
A stranger and exile I wander to-day,
So let me rove on in the shadowy sphere,
And call me not back to the world and its care.

THE OLD FOLKS' CHRISTMAS.

"Draw up to the fire, old woman,
And as the sparks fly away
We'll watch once more together,
The coming of Christmas Day.
It's the seventy-second coming
We've so watched for through life,
As children, friends or lovers;
And sixty as man and wife.

"It does seem hard, old woman,
Not one should be left behind
Out of all we have loved and lost,
Out of all who've been good and kind.
Death's sickle has been o'er busy,
And our branches lopped away,
Only the old and withered trunks
Have been allowed to stay.

"Our boys and girls whose Spring time
  We hoped would support our Fall,
Have been reaped to the Heavenly garner,
  And we have outlived them all.
The merry little children
  Who have played about your knee,
We thought would close our eyelids,
  But God said it might not be.

"E'en our darling, bright-eyed Annie,
  The youngest, last and best,
Just budding into womanhood—
  We've laid her, too, to rest.
Last Christmas she was with us
  So joyous, gay and kind—
Oh, would that we'd been taken,
  And she been left behind!

"It has often soothed our sorrow
  And chased away our pain,
To sit by the dancing fire
  And see Christmas come again;
But now we are, oh, so lonely,
  We can only humbly pray
'Father in thy great mercy
  Suffer us not to stay;

'Thou hast seen fit to leave us
The last of all our race,
To gain Thy Heavenly presence,
To view Thy gracious face;
Grant that the time may shorten
Which Thou hast yet to give,
But also grant, in mercy,
That when we die we live'"
* * * * * *

Hand in hand together
As they'd sat long ago,
The aged couple waited;
Counting the seconds slow,
As creeping round the dial
The minute hand held its way,
Towards the hour which token'd
The coming of Christmas day.

And as each second fleeted
Into time's eternal space,
They felt it brought them nearer
The finish of their race;
And they bowed their heads in silence
While their lips were moved in prayer,
In that heart and soul communion
Only God and his angels hear.

The tall old clock in the corner
The hour of midnight tolled,
Slowly and grandly, it's refrain
Upward and onward rolled.
And the aged heads bent lower,
And the hands were tighter clasped,
As they counted each stroke of the hour,
All to the very last.

Then, as the bells in concert
Rung out in wild delight,
Heralding in the morning
Their spirits took their flight.
No more of weary longing
To be with loved ones 'neath the sod;
They had gone to spend their Christmas
In Heaven with their God.

MUSIC.

There is music in the air,
As in zephyr breeze it blows,
Telling of opening Spring time
Ending the reign of snows.
There is music in the blast,
As in mighty wrath it breaks
Over the lakes and oceans,
Crested with foamy flakes.

There is music in the brooklet
As it trickles to the river;
There is music in the noble stream
Which floweth on for ever.
There is music in the ocean
When in thunder's tone it speaks,
And raiseth up it's haughty crest
In foamcapped, towering peaks.

There is music in a clump of trees
In the calm, still twilight hour,
When every happy little bird
Is flitting to its bower.
There is music in the forest
When the wind, with giant might
Strides fiercely through and leaves
It's pride, all shattered in a night.

There is music all around us
Above and underground,
A solemn voice of warning
In every form and sound.
In every little pebble
We kick away from sight,
There is nature's music ringing
If we only hear aright

God's voice is always near us,
In every sound we hear;
In the loudest roar, or faintest sigh,
That falleth on the ear.
Sometimes in mighty accents
It tells us of His might,
Sometimes in peaceful whispers
It wooes us to His sight.

GHOSTS ON THE WINDOW PANE.

The ghosts of the leaves have come again,
And bloom once more on my window-pane;
In tiny leaflet or slender vine,
Or giant leaves on branches fine
The frost takes shape; in fancy's eye
Like the forest groves of days gone by;
And Summer's glory I see again,
Traced in white on my window pane.

The ghosts of the flowers once more are seen,
And bud anew in the crystal's sheen;
The rose, the lily, and forget-me-not,
And daisies grown in some shelter'd spot;
The buttercup bright, and pansy fair,
Fancy can see all pictured there,
In the ghostly landscape traced in white
On my window-pane by the frost last night.

Fancy again can see the grove
I've wandered through with those I love;
In fancy I again inhale
The perfume sweet of some flow'ry vale,
The ghost of which so deftly drawn
I find on my window-pane at dawn;
Traced as no artists' hand can trace
In all the beauty of nature's grace.

So, when Wintry age shall on me lie,
And my Summer of life has flitted by,
On the glass of memory may there be
Some leaves and flowers traced for me;
Ghostly traces, but memories yet
Of happy days I would not forget;
And thoughts to teach me so to die
That Summer may bloom beyond the sky.

THE CHILD'S GRAVE.

The clear cold air of Christmas-Day
Was resting on the churchyard scene,
When two aged figures bent their way
The snow clad graves and tombs between;
Until they reached a sheltered spot
Beneath a weeping willow's shade,
Where trimly kept and unforgot
An infant's narrow grave was laid.

Only a tiny piece of clay,
Only a little mound of earth,
Only a baby passed away,
And gone back to its mother earth.
Brief was the joy or pain it knew,
Swiftly ran out life's feeble sand,
Little of life's faint breath it drew
Then passed back to its spirit land.

Great was the void it left behind
In the two hearts that loved it so—
Father and mother; who can find
Words in which their grief to show.
It was their first, their only one,
And granted to them late in years,
No more were sent, that one is gone,
And they bedew its grave with tears.

The heads were grey which o'er its grave
Bent down to kiss the unconscious sod,
The hearts were green which humbly prayed
To meet this loved one with their God.
But while they wept a spirit band
Seemed in the air to echo sound,
And tell them of that golden land
Where all the weary's wounds are bound;

To whisper words that he who came
On Christmas day so long ago,
To save the world from sin and shame,
Would heal their grief and quench their woe;
That in the land beyond the sky,
Where peace and joy for ever reign,
Where no tear drop shall dim the eye,
Their darling they shall meet again.

GOD IN NATURE.

Out in the sunlight, the broad burning sunlight,
  I think of God's justice, His power I scan;
I trace in each sunbeam that comes with its bright
    gleam,
  The course of His anger on renegade man.

The sun brightly glowing, seems evermore growing,
  And ready, in anger, to rush from the sky;
Its rays seem to warn me, and caution and learn
    me,
  Of the fate which behind hard, stern justice doth lie.

And then each bright beam doth suddenly seem,
  To be welded and formed into Justice's stern sword;
And the winds seem to breathe "Repent and believe,
  Or dread the just anger and wrath of the Lord."

Out in the moonlight, the calm gentle moonlight,
  I think of God's mercy and pity for men;
And I watch the soft beam, which like silver doth
    seem,
  And calm thoughts and holy come over me then.

Then I call up the story of the Angel of Glory,
  Who came in the moonlight to shepherds of yore;
And told them of Him who would save them from sin
  And guard them from evil and death evermore.

While such thoughts come o'er me, the moon seems
    before me,
  To grow and expand to the home of the blest;
And an angel of lightness sings out through the
    brightness,
  "Come home, thou poor sinner, and fold thee to rest."

Then the thin slender rays seem, to my amaze,
  To form in a ladder which leads to the skies,
And I hear the soft call which, like fairy notes fall,
  "Awake thou worn soul, and on Mercy arise."

Thus whether by sunlight, or under the starlight,
  God's attributes ever before us are shown;
His Justice, bright gleaming, like sunlight is stream-
    ing,
  While the moon in mild Mercy, leads up to His
    Throne.

THE DYING CHILD.

But how can she be dead, nurse,
What do you mean by dead;
For good people can never die
So mamma always said;
And mamma never told a fib
She was so good and true,
Why has she gone away nurse,
And left me here with you?

You say that she's in Heaven, nurse,
But how am I to know;
And why can't I be with her,
I'm sure I want to go.
You say she looks down on me
With loving, watchful eye;
If so, why can't I see her
However hard I try?

You say the stars are eyes, nurse
Of dead ones whom we love,
Who nightly keep their silent watch
Upon us from above.
If so, I'm sure the evening star
My mamma's eye must be,
For never mind which way I turn
It always looks at me.

So lay me by the window, nurse,
Where I can watch its ray;
And while it's shining on me
I'll lift my hands and pray,
That God will kindly take me too
Into his Heavenly rest,
And let me go to sleep once more
Upon my mother's breast.

I heard the doctor say, nurse,
I was about to die,
Oh, how I hope I soon may be
With my mamma on high;
And when I am a star, nurse,
In the Heaven above so blue,
I'll try to shine bright every night
Just to look down on you.

When you see a little star,
With the evening star shall be,
Nestling quite close beside it
You'll know that star is me;
And I'll ask mamma to help me
To watch o'er you, and pray
For the one who's been so kind to me,
Since she was called away.

So do not cry for me, nurse,
I shall be happier far up there,
Sleeping again in mamma's arms
And floating in the air,

See how the star grows larger
And wings come long and bright;
I see my mamma's face now
So nursey dear, good night.

THE FACTORY GIRL.

She wasn't the least bit pretty,
And only the least bit gay;
And she walked with a firm elastic tread,
In a business-like kind of way.
Her dress was of coarse, brown woollen,
Plainly but neatly made,
Trimmed with some common ribbon
Or cheaper kind of braid;
And a hat with a broken feather,
And shawl of a modest plaid.

Her face seemed worn and weary,
And traced with lines of care,
As her nut-brown tresses blew aside
In the keen December air;
Yet she was not old, scarce twenty,
And her form was full and sleek,
But her heavy eye, and tired step,
Seemed of wearisome toil to speak;
She worked as a common factory girl
For two dollars and a half a week.

Ten hours a day of labor
In a close, ill-lighted room;
Machinery's buzz for music,
Waste gas for sweet perfume;
Hot stifling vapors in summer,
Chill draughts on a winter's day,
No pause for rest or pleasure
On pain of being sent away;
So ran her civilized serfdom—
Four cents an hour the pay.

"A fair day's work," say the masters,
And "a fair day's pay," say the men;
There's a strike—a rise in wages,
What effect to the poor girl then?
A harder struggle than ever
The honest path to keep;
And so sink a little lower,
Some humbler home to seek;
For living is dearer—her wages,
Two dollars and a half a week.

A man gets thrice the money,
But then "a man's a man,
"And a woman surely can't expect
"To earn as much as he can."
Of his hire the laborer's worthy,

Be that laborer who it may;
If a woman can do a man's work
She should have a man's full pay,
Not to be left to starve—or sin—
On forty cents a day.

Two dollars and a half to live on,
Or starve on, if you will;
Two dollars and a half to dress on,
And a hungry mouth to fill;
Two dollars and a half to lodge on
In some wretched hole or den,
Where crowds are huddled together,
Girls, and women, and men;
If she sins to escape her bondage
Is there room for wonder then.

PLEASANT REVERIES.

'Tis sweet from earth to wander,
　Through fancy's realm to roam;
On former joys to ponder,
　Or build a future home.
How old scenes rise before us,
　And fill the visioned sight;
Old mem'ries come back o'er us
　With rapturous delight.
Some long forgotten feeling
　Comes filling us with joy,
And o'er the senses stealing
　Makes bliss without alloy.

Or far into the future
  Is cast our dreaming gaze,
And a new born scene, far happier,
  Arises from its haze.
We hear the rippling fountain,
  We smell the balmy flowers;
We see the stately mountain,
  And cool Arcadian bowers;
In fancy's mind we picture
  Perpetual realms of bliss,
When fond hearts beat together
  And seal love with a kiss.

THE END

www.ingramcontent.com/pod-product-compliance
Lightning Source LLC
Chambersburg PA
CBHW031351230426
43670CB00006B/505